"*Running on Empty* is more than a book title; it has become a way of life. But there is another, much better way. Fil Anderson points us to it with grace, thoughtfulness, and style. Read him and be filled again."

—JOHN ORTBERG, author of *Everybody's Normal Till You Get to Know Them*

"This book is for those of us who have found it easier to take care of our schedule than to take care of our soul. For the unfortunate majority who keep running because we don't know how to stop, Fil Anderson provides a compelling road map home where we can finally stop and snuggle up in the arms of God."

—MICHAEL YACONELLI, author of *Messy Spirituality: God's Annoying Love for Imperfect People* and *Dangerous Wonder: The Adventure of Childlike Faith*

"Fil Anderson invites you to discover the difference between believing that God is love and experiencing the love of God. As the author makes clear, it's the difference in life and death for your soul."

—CRAIG BARNES, author of *When God Interrupts*

"*Running on Empty* is an oasis for those of us who allow a life of busyness to drive us toward emptiness. Fil Anderson's honesty and vulnerability can lead us all toward the One who fills us eternally."

—DENNY RYDBERG, president of Young Life

"What a fresh voice Fil Anderson brings to all of us who struggle to *be* with Jesus and not just *do* for him. This book draws me back to the wonder of the gospel—which is the best recommendation I could give any book."

—PAULA RINEHART, author of *Strong Women, Soft Hearts* and *Sex and the Soul of a Woman*

"Fil Anderson has written a deeply personal story of his own walk with God. In doing so, he is brave and caring enough to share with us many practical ways to deepen our own walk."

—BOB BUFORD, founder of Leadership Network and author of *Halftime: Changing Your Game Plan from Success to Significance*

"*Running on Empty* is written by someone who can recognize emptiness because he has known both emptiness and fullness. This book is inspiring and yet practical, anecdotal and yet big-picture, traditional and yet contemporary American. Enjoy its fullness."

—RICHARD ROHR, O.F.M., Center for Action and Contemplation, Albuquerque, New Mexico

"Unless we learn the lessons in this book, we will dry up in building God's kingdom. Fil Anderson shows us how to keep our own souls refreshed. A *must*-read for all those in ministry!"

—REV. JOHN YATES and SUSAN ALEXANDER YATES, coauthors of *Building a Home Full of Grace* and *Character Matters: Raising Kids with Values That Last*

"This book is destined to become a classic for those who are serious about learning to love Christ and wanting to know they are loved by him."

—HOWARD DAYTON, CEO of Crown Financial Ministries

"With simplicity and integrity, Fil Anderson poses questions and offers challenges and possibilities to assist readers in the exploration of their own stories. One gets the sense of Fil, the spiritual director, standing at the door praying for readers as they enter the sacred space of their exploration."

—ROSE MARY DOUGHERTY, SSND, author of *Group Spiritual Direction: Community for Discernment* and editor of *The Experience of Group Spiritual Direction*

"If you're caught in the rat race, at the edge of burnout, or even too busy to notice, *Running on Empty* offers help and hope. Here is a Christian response to the drivenness of modern American culture, a response that offers both inspiration and down-to-earth wisdom."

—GERALD MAY, author of *Will and Spirit* and *Addiction and Grace*

"*Running on Empty* offers hope that we can learn to accept the love of God in our brokenness. Our busyness can be quieted, and our souls can learn to be at peace in the face of God's unrestrained love."

—DEVLIN DONALDSON, The Elevation Group; coauthor of *Pinocchio Nation*

"Fil Anderson provides fellow travelers with practical ideas and tools for walking the journey with and toward Christ. This deeply personal book gives believers like me hope of moving from religious compulsions to a fresh relationship with the Lord."

—TOM WILSON, president/CEO of Leadership Network

RUNNING ON
EMPTY

Contemplative Spirituality for Overachievers

FIL ANDERSON

WATERBROOK
PRESS

Running on Empty
Published by WaterBrook Press
2375 Telstar, Suite 160
Colorado Springs, Colorado 80920
A division of Random House, Inc.

The author has made every effort to ensure the truthfulness of the stories and anecdotes in this book. In a few instances, names and identifying details have been changed to protect the privacy of the persons involved.

ISBN 1-57856-834-X

Library of Congress Cataloging-in-Publication Data
Anderson, Fil.
    Running on empty : contemplative spirituality for overachievers /
Fil Anderson.— 1st ed.
        p. cm.
Includes bibliographical references.
    ISBN 1-57856-834-X
    1. Spiritual life—Christianity. I. Title.
    BV4501.3.A525 2004
    248.4—dc22

                                                            2003017521

Printed in the United States of America
2004

10 9 8 7 6 5 4 3 2

To
Lucie,
Meredith, Will, and Lee
this book is warmly and gratefully dedicated.
Thank you for loving me. Especially when I was *running on empty*.

CONTENTS

FOREWORD

We drunks in Alcoholics Anonymous have a saying: "Coincidence is God's way of protecting his anonymity." The origin of the saying is obscure, and no respectable sot would lay claim to its authorship. But whatever the source of the *coincidence* definition, I have no doubt that my initial meeting with Fil Anderson was by divine appointment. In retrospect, there is simply no other explanation.

Sixteen years ago neither of us was supposed to be in Vail, Colorado, a playground for the rich and famous. Nonetheless, one of the sumptuous ski resorts there hosts an annual healing conference that attracts primarily charismatic Christians from around the United States and Europe and from a potpourri of countries from other continents.

The three regularly featured speakers are Francis and Judith MacNutt, widely known for their teachings on healing, and—no longer now—the late Tommy Tyson, a dynamic evangelist. One fall Tommy took ill, and I was fetched as a replacement. My motive for accepting the invitation was pure—purely vainglorious. I wanted to be identified with the superstars on the circuit. Hungry for approval and acceptance, I saw Vail as a venue to glory, and I concluded that a few days of luxurious living in paradise would not quench my spiritual fervor.

At the time Fil was a regional director of Young Life living in Greensboro, North Carolina. His cluttered personal life and flourishing ministry left no time for spiritual retreats, especially a charismatic conference, yet here he was. Reared in the evangelical tradition, he did not view praying in tongues as, to put it politely, his cup of tea. However, his longing for a saner pace was so intense he was willing to try anything.

So two desperately insecure men, total strangers to each other, showed up in Vail. During her first presentation, Judith MacNutt emphasized the importance of spiritual direction and recommended that each attendee seek out a mentor. My door was open, Fil popped in, and one of the few deep friendships I have ever had in my life began that sunlit morning.

In this achingly beautiful book, Fil tells my story by sharing his own. He had been hooked on approval since infancy. The interior urgency to make his mark as a spiritual leader in the adult world bore unintended but horrific consequences. Fil threw himself again and again into a whirlwind of activity that garnered praise and admiration from the senior Young Life staff as well as kudos from countless parents and kids. He became a player in the kingdom enterprise, gained the world, and lost himself along the way. Physically exhausted and spiritually demoralized, he then began the inward journey.

The raw honesty of this book is jarring: "I have been ripped apart by the relentlessly competing demands of my job and home, wife and children, friends and family who persistently ask for more than I've ever felt capable of giving. My hopes for the future have been haunted by the blunders in my past. My desperate longing to get my life right has been dogged by the nagging fear that it will never, ever happen, given the obvious fact that I am hopelessly flawed."

Honesty is a precious commodity seldom found in the world or in the church. Like the alcoholic who denies he has a drinking problem, many of us have deluded ourselves for so long that dishonesty and self-deception have become not only an acceptable but a necessary way of life. *Esse quam videri* read the coat of arms of early church father Gregory Nazianzen: "to be rather than appear to be." Appearing to be is now normative; sham and pretense comprise enough to get by; and in the succinctly exquisite words of Carl Jung: "Neurosis is always a substitute for legitimate suffering."[1]

Dishonesty allows my false self, the impostor who is the slick, sick, and subtle impersonator of true self, to engage in life on a fraudulent basis. Fil writes, "I had learned to impersonate someone I wanted to be but had never figured out how to be an authentically spiritual person." Flagrant signs of dishonesty in my own life include the following: I grow fearful when a more gifted writer swipes my baton, cynical when feedback is negative, paranoid when threatened, worried that I am worried, fitful when challenged, and distraught when defeated.

Obviously, emotions that are not expressed cannot be fixed. Frozen anger leads to resentment; repressed resentment leads to consuming guilt; guilt induces depression. Repressed persons are often depressed persons—as I knew when I found myself taking an antidepressant. The denial, displacement, or repression of feelings is blatant dishonesty and leads to a loss of integrity.

In an uncanny paradox, Fil's scorching honesty and humble transparency ravish the heart of Jesus Christ.

The emphasis in this book on the indispensable importance of silence and solitude is timely and pointed. Jesus teaches that we should go into a closet to pray. In contemplation we return to our naked, poor self and discover who we are apart from the role we play. When we take ourselves too seriously, we identify with image, with what we think we are, with our reputation and the applause and compliments of others. Silent solitude liberates the pray-er from the tyranny of the approval and disapproval of others.

Reading Fil's story reveals how breakdowns often lead to breakthroughs. The breakthrough into honesty on the journey happens when we come to value the approval of God more than the approval of others. Our spoken and written words become simple and direct. As Fil observes, our prayer becomes primarily silent listening as we let ourselves be loved in our tawdry hubris, dishonesty, and brokenness.

We express feelings without inhibition and anxiety, and our hearts relax in the presence of unrestricted love.

To the harried and the unharried, I pray that *Running on Empty* ministers to your heart in the profound way that it has blessed mine.

BRENNAN MANNING
New Orleans

PREFACE

Nearly two decades ago a fifteen-minute conversation changed my life. I was attending a conference and had signed up to meet with one of the speakers for something announced as "spiritual direction." I didn't know what spiritual direction was, but I did know that I enjoyed dropping the names of the well-known Christian authors and speakers I would occasionally meet. I didn't expect anything significant to happen during such a brief encounter in this spiritual equivalent of getting a baseball autographed. All I wanted was a superficial conversation and a personally signed copy of his new book so I could brag that Brennan Manning and I were friends.

Before this encounter the words of Jesus that "where two or three are gathered in my name, I am there among them" (Matthew 18:20) held no special significance for me. Yet on that afternoon I experienced the reality of his divine presence through Brennan Manning, whose words exposed the truth of the condition of my soul.

"We are not alone," he assured me. Out of love, Jesus had chosen to be there with us. "Don't be distracted by my presence," Brennan said, "but know that we are with the One who loves you as you are, not as you should be, since you will never be the person you should be." His strange words were somehow comforting. And they set me up for what would happen next.

He began asking questions about a part of me I had not considered for quite some time. "Tell me about the condition of your soul," Brennan asked. Then he waited for a response. I was clueless. How could I tell this stranger about a part of me with which I was so unfamiliar? To squirm free from the silence, I began babbling about the most maddening aspect of my life: the frantic, out-of-control, frenzied

pace I couldn't seem to escape. I told him about my fatigue and emptiness. I described how overwhelming my life was, even on the very best
of days. After listening for a while, he made the statement that
changed my life: "Fil, you seem dreadfully close to losing touch with
the Jesus you so desperately want others to know."

Never had words pierced my heart as these did. This stranger had
looked inside me and was exposing a truth about myself to which I
had been totally oblivious. Later, when I was alone, I wondered, *Was
this Jesus speaking into my life?* For quite some time I'd had a gnawing
sensation that certain things in my life were out of control. But there
had been no time to analyze the problem, its cause, or what might
result if I couldn't rein in the chaos. In the process of going in four different directions at the same time, constantly striving and always busy,
I had lost my soul. Then on that day at that conference, speaking with
this holy man, I began to hope I just might have some worth beyond
being busy so others would notice my achievements.

The chapters of this book lay out in vivid, painful detail my
struggle with busyness. They expose the lie of busyness as the world's
most effective strategy to keep us estranged from God. They explain
common and dangerous blind spots: Why am I unable to say no when
asked to take on a new responsibility that I know will spread me too
thin? Why do I have such a need to be needed? Why do I resent the
steady assault on my time yet live in constant fear that there will not
be enough to do to keep me busy?

After my first conversation with Brennan, I set out on a spiritual
journey that redefined my view of God. By gaining a right perspective
on God, my view of others, myself, and all that I do in life also was
reshaped.

Somewhere along the way I discovered that hearing the confessions of others had a way of putting me in touch with the hidden
things in my own life, things that needed to be confessed. So in many
ways this book is a work of confession. I hope my story will speak to

your story. Hear my confessions about my struggle with busyness and discover for yourself the soul-shaping truth and bone-deep hope that you have incalculable worth to Jesus and to those whom God has put in your life. Follow me into the hidden harbors of the heart, where fear, loneliness, and resentment drop anchor. Celebrate with me the ways the Spirit of God can blow through our lives with hurricane force, breaking us free from the distorted images of inadequacy that need to be healed. Hopefully, you will find that force of God's Spirit that longs to blow through your life—removing the debris of whatever hinders you, freeing you to live in the center of your true place as the object of God's relentless love.

If you are too busy for your own good and unwilling to face the deeper issues that drive your life, then please put this book aside, at least for now. However, if you are willing to face squarely the underlying causes that drive you to live this way, being beaten senseless by external demands while inside you are withering away, then I urge you to read on. Today is the day to finally shout "Enough!"

ACKNOWLEDGMENTS

Countless times during the two years I concentrated on writing this book, folks asked, "How long has it taken you to write your book?" Often I've responded with the simple answer, "Fifty-two years," which has been the length of my life thus far.

Who I am is what I have written. In the process, I've realized that being authentic and sharing those parts of me that I believe we all have in common is terribly complex and demanding. I would never have dared to attempt this challenge without the encouragement and help of many people. If it's true that it takes a village to raise a child, I've learned that it takes at least a village for me to write a book.

It is my heart's most sincere desire to acknowledge the people who have helped me. Each in his or her unique way has helped make this goal of authenticity more achievable. It is this wonderful group of people I wish to recognize and thank:

The Notorious Sinners, who have loved me "without caution, regret, boundary, or breaking point": Gene, Lou, Devlin, John, Mickey, Butch, Alan, Paul, John, Brennan, Ed, Paul, John Peter, Bob, and Mike.

Kathy Helmers, for daring to speak truthfully and for believing in my voice even when I had lost it. For being so much more than my agent, for becoming a soul mate and taking such a huge risk with me. I will never be able to repay you.

The Journey Resources Board of Directors and Advisors, for their relentless devotion and confidence in me.

Jerry Clark and Jonathan Smith, who with uncommon patience and kindness read and reread my manuscript, graciously offering with candor their priceless editorial suggestions.

The entire Young Life community, particularly those who were and remain my mentors and friends.

My Friday men's group—Mike, Rod, and David—for providing me a safe place to both discover and become the person I truly am.

Those people, for whom my admiration is immense, who were willing to read my manuscript and offer generous endorsements.

Lucie and my couples group—Mike and Susie Fowler, Bill and Joann Goans, Johnny and Sue Wilson—for offering us a place to shed our tears, discuss our hurts, expose our failures, celebrate our joys and successes, and work at some of the changes reflected in this book.

The people who are Grace Community Church and Westminster Presbyterian Church, for encouraging me by their example, strengthening me by their prayers, and providing me with both a launching pad and safe place to land and refuel.

Vic and Susan Cochran and Bob and Anne Rodman, for providing me the perfect space in which to write and for constantly encouraging me along the way.

Lucie's and my parents, siblings, and their families, for loving me and constantly offering their support.

The magnificent people at the Shalem Institute for Spiritual Formation, for playing such a vital role in my spiritual formation, especially Rose Mary Dougherty, Tilden Edwards, and Gerald May.

The influential thinking of so many more-gifted writers than I, whose profound insights contributed incalculably to the writing of this book, on whose shoulders I am privileged to stand, and to whom I owe an unpayable debt.

Brennan Manning, for his unrivaled friendship, mentoring, and willingness to write the foreword for this work.

The monks of Mepkin Abbey and the many others who have modeled a life of utter devotion to God and have companioned me as spiritual director.

And finally, Dorothy Kuyath, for the photograph on the cover.

Part 1

A PATH OF
DESTRUCTION

1

CONFESSIONS OF A RECOVERING WORK ADDICT

Speeding Up While the Tank Runs Dry

Noise and words and frenzied, hectic schedules
dull our senses, closing our ears to His still, small voice
and making us numb to His touch.
— CHARLES SWINDOLL, *Intimacy with the Almighty*

Running on empty." Had I died fifteen years ago, this is how I most likely would have been remembered. I hated being harried and hassled by life's demands and pressures, but I loved being in demand.

Late at night, while Lucie and our children slept, I would lie awake fearing that I had come to the end of my rope. My despair was the by-product of the life I had created for my family and myself. It had not appeared overnight. What finally came crashing down was the result of fifteen years of relentless striving. While attempting to enable others to encounter God, I had succumbed to the power of my compulsions and illusions. The lifestyle that appeared to enhance my friendship with God had become instead a terrible threat. What had driven me to speak more *about* God than *with* God? What had driven me from one event to another, one project to another, one relationship to another? Why could I never say no?

These questions would resurface during the rare moments of calm and quiet in my life. Perhaps in the daylight hours I was trying to hide from memories buried deep within. Perhaps I was more interested in the approval of people than in the love of God. Perhaps I was sinking beneath the weight of an image—that of having it all together—which was too heavy for me to project any longer. Late at night, as my family slept, I couldn't keep hiding. The questions came unbidden, and I knew time was about to run out.

I was more than busy; I was exhausted. At night I was restless—too many of the day's activities would loop through my brain. And the following morning it was all I could do to drag myself out of bed to face the day. I was running on grit and adrenaline. For quite some time I had loved having every moment crammed with activity. More specifically, it was the fuel on which I ran. I loved being in demand. But now I was running on empty.

UNREQUITED LONGINGS

As I reflect on life back then, I'm reminded of the tragic death of professional golfer Payne Stewart and the friends who died with him. Had I been standing on the tarmac as their plane taxied to the runway for takeoff, I would have undoubtedly been impressed with the jet's sleekness and style. Looking up, after takeoff, I would have commented on how nice it would be to travel in such comfort. I would also have been unaware that something was tragically wrong on the inside of that powerful aircraft.

Departing central Florida, the Learjet flew a ghostly journey halfway across the country, its windows iced over and its occupants apparently incapacitated, before spiraling nosefirst into a grassy field. Everyone aboard was killed. The Lear 35 may have suddenly lost cabin pressure soon after taking off for Dallas, government officials said later. The attempts of air traffic controllers to make radio contact were unsuccessful.

Fighter jets were sent after the plane and followed it for much of its flight, but they were unable to help. The military pilots drew close and noticed no structural damage, but they were unable to see into the Learjet because its windows were frosted over. The temperature inside must have dropped well below freezing.

Apparently set on autopilot, the plane cruised fourteen hundred miles over the nation's midsection, across half a dozen states. Authorities say the plane was "porpoising," fluctuating between twenty-two thousand feet and fifty-one thousand feet. The aircraft presumably ran out of fuel some four hours after it took off.

Stewart's wife, Tracey, desperately tried to reach her husband on his cellular phone while she followed the nightmarish drama on television. There was no answer, and finally the jet crashed in a grassy field.[1]

This tragic image serves well as a metaphor of my life some fifteen years ago. To the casual onlooker, my life appeared quite good. I was flying high. My work among high school students in Greensboro, North Carolina, was highly praised. And it wasn't all for show. It was clear that God was working; people's lives were changing.

But something was wrong inside me. My life—like the Learjet on autopilot—had become a ghostly journey as I maintained a deadly course with an incapacitated soul. My ability to see clearly had become nil, outside efforts to get me to change course were refused, and my last bit of fuel was being depleted. I was obsessed with helping others have the kind of relationship with God that I had never known.

I wasn't able to name my longings or express my yearnings. My life was filled with doing things for God rather than pursuing intimacy with God. I had perfected busyness but failed miserably at stillness. I worked constantly, averaging seventy to eighty hours per week, but I didn't have a clue who my Boss was. Although I knew facts and ideas about Jesus, I didn't know what it meant to be his friend. I had confidence in my ability to do the work of God, but I was clueless when it came to letting God work in me. I could talk easily with others about Jesus, but I knew nothing about how to sit still long enough for Jesus to talk with me. I was comfortable around others who knew God, but the thought of being alone with God was enough to keep me occupied with the demands of ministry. The idea of sitting alone in a room with God made me nervous.

In my deepest parts I knew that God was everywhere. Yet often I wondered and even doubted whether God was in my spirit. I had traded God for other gods that were more to my liking. At least they fed my ego in ways God seemed uninterested in doing. I worshiped at the altar of adulation. My soul was hemorrhaging, but I wasn't yet ready to apply a tourniquet.

When asked how I was doing, I would often respond, "So busy I don't know if I'm coming or going." It's a pity that I was deaf to the truth in my own responses.

I had become like a child playing on a merry-go-round, laughing and having the best of times. But occasionally the constant spinning would take its toll. Like a child, I would become queasy and dizzy and cry to get off. When I finally did stop, my head would be spinning, and I would wonder, *How did I ever get this way?*

SETTING THE STAGE

The soul-deadening pace of my life was not new. The stage had been set long before.

During my freshman year in college I was invited to be the part-time youth pastor in my home church. I was an eighteen-year-old with a growing love for God and an increasing awareness of God's love for me. I was also desperately in need of the recognition that my job provided but completely unprepared for the weight of expectations that were placed on me. Even now I sometimes wonder what the leadership of that church was thinking. At other times I wonder, *What was I thinking?*

I was in over my head, but I would rather die than admit that, so I learned a simple lesson that seemed to provide the direction I needed: Just stay busy. In the church, as long as you appear busy, people rarely question your knowledge or effectiveness. They assume wherever there is a cloud of dust, meaningful activity must be just ahead of it. So I started kicking up perpetual clouds of dust.

As I kept busy, I also learned that ceaseless activity earned me tremendous praise. Desperate for recognition and approval, I worked even harder. But by the end of my first year I was suffering from fatigue and constantly feeling overwhelmed and inadequate. But I kept at it, and by the end of my second year I got a promotion. I was named the pastor of a fledgling church. At age twenty-one I was unable to distinguish between my activity and my identity—and so my activity determined my identity.

I lived in constant fear that I would be exposed for what I truly was—inadequate. If others realized how incompetent I was, my illusory importance would be exposed and my identity would be threatened. I had to maintain the facade, and the weight of responsibility was killing me.

I returned to my apartment one Sunday afternoon and fell across my bed and sobbed. "What if someone discovers that most of my sermon was copied from a book of sermons? I am such an impostor! God, I hate what I've become!"

I fell asleep, then awoke in a fog of despair. "What will I say in tonight's service? What lies will I have to tell to maintain the reputation I've carefully crafted?" My days were not lived but endured. I had strained for so long to live up to the image I had fabricated—now I was being tyrannized by it.

Desperate for help, I looked in the most anonymous place I knew:

the Christian book section of a nearby bookstore. I began reading about Christians living victoriously. They were overcoming fears, doubts, and feelings of inadequacy. Far from being a source of encouragement, these stories only increased my fears and multiplied my doubts. Why was my life so dark? What was wrong with my faith that I couldn't live above my circumstances? Soon I began to shame myself for being so weak. Self-hatred became the order of the day, every day.

THE FACADE CRUMBLES

In late winter a streptococcus pneumoniae bacterium invaded my badly suppressed immune system. Laid low by pneumonia, I worried what people would think. I needed to return to my responsibilities as quickly as possible. So after five days I got back to work, determined to demonstrate my full commitment to ministry. And before long I relapsed into a severe case of double pneumonia.

The American Lung Association reports that, in pneumonia:

> The tissue of part of a lobe of the lung, an entire lobe, or even most of the lung's five lobes become completely filled with liquid. The infection quickly spreads through the bloodstream and the whole body is invaded.
>
> The external signs of this sudden bacterial onset include shaking chills, chattering teeth, severe chest pain, and a cough that heaves up the darkness of the deep. A person's temperature may rise as high as 105 degrees F. The patient sweats profusely, and breathing and pulse rate increase rapidly. Lips and nail beds may have a bluish color due to lack of oxygen in the blood. A patient's mental state may be confused or delirious.[2]

A confused or delirious mental state. I didn't know at the time what this disease was doing to my insides. But on the outside, the parts of me that were seen by others, I knew the facade covering my inadequacy was wearing frighteningly thin.

By midspring what I feared most finally occurred. Looking back, I realize it was what author Sheldon Vanauken described as a "severe mercy."[3] The ominous fear and fatigue that I had kept hidden led me into a state of utter exhaustion and depression. I wept uncontrollably. No longer could I hold up the mask. As frightening as this was to me, it was also very liberating.

My parents were in panic. The pastor who had been my mentor was in despair. Knowing no other place to turn, I admitted myself into the psychiatric unit of a local hospital. Those of you who have traveled this path will recognize some of your own story in mine. Those of you who have never been this close to the edge might find the nakedness of this episode helpful or possibly frightening. As I try to tell you what happened, please understand that it's an indescribable journey.

I will never forget telling my parents good-bye and stepping into an elevator with a kind nurse who paid me the service of not talking as we rode to the floor housing the psychiatric unit. When I was shown to my room, just looking around and noticing the precautions that had been taken for my protection was enough to depress me. A person wanting to do him or herself harm would find it a daunting challenge in that room. A nurse appeared and asked if she could look through my belongings. When she left, she took with her my belt, shoes, a small pair of scissors, and my razor.

For two weeks I lived behind locked doors with other deeply troubled and disturbed persons. Although to you this might sound like a nightmare, to me it was the safest, most caring place I had been for quite some time. At long last there was no one I needed to care for or impress. Instead, there were people who actually wanted to care for *me*. They assured me that feeling broken was neither wrong nor a sign of weakness. They urged me to rest. They spoke of my great value at a point in my life when I could do absolutely nothing to prove my worth. They loved me. And in the safety behind those locked doors and barred windows, and among other broken souls, I began to face my own brokenness, fears, and inadequacy.

My doctor was a gentle but strong man, the son of missionaries. On our last morning together, he tried as best he could to explain what had happened to me. He recalled a day when he was water skiing with a friend who was known for practical jokes. This friend foolishly thought it would be funny to keep pulling an exhausted skier around the lake. At long last the friend brought the boat parallel to the shore. My doctor, who was the desperate, exhausted skier, released the rope and coasted toward the shore. Perhaps like me, he had been too embarrassed and afraid to admit his fatigue sooner by dropping the ski rope.

As he slowed, his skis settled deeper into the water, breaking his forward motion. That's when he fell facefirst into shallow water. With his face submerged, his brain told his body to respond, to turn over so he could breathe. But there was no response. He could not muster the strength to move even his head. As he began to lose consciousness, he realized he might very well drown right where he was. Yet his body was physically incapable of turning over, even if it meant death. Fortunately, someone on the beach came running to his rescue.

The doctor explained what by then was obvious. My incessant activity had worn me down to the point that I was too tired to rescue myself. The doctor went on to talk about his missionary father, a man who spent his adult life loving God and others as he loved himself. He described the rhythm of his father's life as "graceful" and his way of treating others, and himself, as "gentle." He urged me to live the rest of my life believing God's love for me was not contingent on my performance. His final words to me were wise and true: "God will never love you any more or less because of anything you manage, or fail, to achieve."

I clung to the words of this kind doctor, and for the first time in my young, harried life I learned a lesson that I desperately needed. And then I got busy and quickly forgot the lifesaving words.

The Pattern Repeats

After college I joined the staff of Young Life, an international ministry to middle school and high school students. I began a career that was to be as exciting as it was rewarding, a life filled with risks and adventure. How I wish I had internalized the lessons I learned in the safety of the hospital. As I threw myself into my new ministry, I once again lost the ability to distinguish between my work and my self. As one close friend explained, "On the surface you appear like a swan graciously gliding along, but beneath the surface you're paddling like a man possessed to get ahead."

I was *filled* and *unfulfilled.* I constantly overcommitted myself. Most troubling was the discomfort I experienced whenever I wasn't busy. This obsession grew to the point that some of my busiest days were the infrequent days I took off. Once again busyness became my identity. How others appraised my work (and consequently appraised me) became the single most important thing in my life.

More enslaving than my occupation were my preoccupations. My mind was consumed with all sorts of what-ifs. What if they don't like me? What if the message I present is not applauded? What if they discover that the love of God I speak of doesn't ring true with my own experience? What if those who think I'm kind and gentle speak to my wife or children and discover how I behave at home? I obsessed over what I would say and what I would do if the things I feared actually occurred. Ultimately my occupation and preoccupations filled my life, and in the process I hindered the Spirit of God from moving freely in me, renewing my life with every beat of God's heart.

While I worried about how I'd ever be able to live up to the expectations imposed on me by others and mostly by myself, I lived with a deep sense of loneliness, fear, frustration, and disappointment. While always busy and usually productive, I rarely felt satisfied, at peace, or at home with myself. As a natural consequence of my feelings of isolation, I was often resentful, afraid, and angry. The saddest part was that I had no idea where these feelings were coming from. And even if I had wanted to explore their origins, there never seemed to be time to step back and allow the feelings to fully surface.

A deadly pattern developed: My body would fall apart whenever I broke away from the constant activity, often around holidays and vacations. On one occasion, my wife, Lucie, and I had just arrived in our hometown of Wilmington, North Carolina, for a week at the beach. Stopping off at my parents' home to get the key to a friend's beach house, I began feeling the first symptoms of the flu. We never made it to the beach. Instead, I spent the week in bed, suffering a miserable bout with the flu, but also a bout with my anger and disappointment. After a few of these holiday breakdowns, my family began to notice the pattern, saying, "It must be the holidays. Fil has the flu."

My lifestyle was making me sick, but I kept up the same insane pace. On occasion, though, I would encounter something that made me question the way I was living.

I Get a Clue

I was on retreat, in the chill and deadness of winter, when I began to feel something different, a wake-up call that opened my eyes to how my true self contrasted with the frenzied rhythm of my life. After several days of quiet and rest, I called home and told Lucie, "I'd give anything for a video recording of myself to send you. I am being more 'me' than I've ever been before. When I'm eating a meal, I no longer hurry. I even put my fork down between bites and enjoy tasting my food. When I'm walking, I walk slowly and quietly. My voice is softer and my words are fewer. I notice things in nature and in the lives of others that I don't recall paying attention to before. I'm more content to sit and listen to God when I pray. The strangest thing of all is how 'at home' I am with myself."

Perhaps like the prodigal son, in the chill and deadness of this winter of my soul I was "coming to my senses," coming home to the person God intended me to be. Finally, after so much heartache, I had a clue about the sort of life God had mercifully planned for me.

On that retreat I read the classic *A Testament of Devotion* by Thomas R. Kelly, a Quaker. As Kelly was describing how God designed us to live, his words fell on my heart like rain in a desert. I followed Kelly as he described how living with "remarkable power and peace and serenity, of integration and confidence and simplified multiplicity" is truly possible, on the condition that we must really *want* to live with "remarkable power and peace and serenity, of integration and confidence and simplified multiplicity."[4] As he offered up this hopeful perspective, I could see the striking contrast between my empty life and the promise of a life of peace. I could see that each misfit part of my soul was sewn to the others with one common thread: distractions, keeping me from hearing the true voice of God. I had heeded God's voice before, though briefly, and during those times my life was filled with a remarkable stability. But mostly I was too distracted and consumed with activity to notice the quiet Voice. My deafness produced a life without peace.

By and large, Quakers are busy people. They would, however, be among the first to recognize how vital it is to have periods of disengagement, even from the activities that express their ongoing commitment to care for people. The particular gift Quakers offer is the awareness of and attention to this deep center of living, where the anxious demands of life are integrated, where saying yes or no to a request or demand can be spoken with quiet assurance. We'll revisit and develop some of these themes in later chapters.

The Problem Is Deeper

The peace and sanity promised in Kelly's book made me aware that the problem was deeper than my addiction to busyness. Had I stopped to ask Jesus about my constant activity, I don't believe he would have tried to pull me away from all the activities, events, and people that summed up my life. I don't imagine Jesus would have said the things I was doing were unimportant. Nor would he have suggested that I withdraw to a life of isolation and quiet contemplation far from the struggles that were burying me.

Instead, Jesus would have nudged me to shift the center of effort in my life, to refocus the center of my attention, to adjust, not abandon, my life's values. I believe Jesus would have urged me to not be so "worried and distracted by many things" and believe him that "there is need of only one thing" (Luke 10:41-42). Through my frustration and disappointment, Jesus was telling me that he wanted me to live in the world but to live differently. He was calling me to live firmly rooted in the center of all things. The change Jesus was calling forth was not a change in activities, contacts, or pace but rather a change of my heart. What he had said to others before, he was now saying to me: "Strive for his kingdom, and these things will be given to you as well" (Luke 12:31). Jesus was helping me to understand that when my heart is set on lots of things, my heart is divided.

In this new light of winter I began to pay closer attention to the life of Jesus. For the first time I recognized how single-minded and centered he was. It was obvious that Jesus lived an extremely busy life. All I had to do was pay attention to his preaching, teaching, healing, and interacting with opponents and friends to see how hard it was for him to remain focused on the "one necessary thing." However, and this is crucial, his busyness never threatened the one thing that mattered most.

Although busy, Jesus wasn't trying to reach some selfish goal he had set or allowed others to impose. To the contrary, he was concerned with only one thing: doing the will of God. We see this from his first recorded words in the temple ("Did you not know that I must be in my Father's house?" [Luke 2:49]) to his last words on the cross ("Father, into Your hands I commit My spirit" [Luke 23:46, NASB]). He claimed, "The Son can do nothing on his own, but only what he sees the Father doing" (John 5:19). I began thinking, *If the Son of God recognized the need to be this deliberate in his devotion, what about me? Can I really afford to be any less intentional in my devotion to God?*

Filled with an encouragement to make the life of God's Spirit within and around me the center of all I think, say, and do, I began the journey toward discovering how to focus my heart on the things that matter most to God. Like others before me who had confronted their own crises of faith, I began to ponder, *Is there within me, beneath all of life's surface issues, a quiet stream that flows continually from the heart of God? Is there a solid place to which my life is riveted and from which I can reach out to others with kindness and compassion?*

My crisis had been much more than a cluster of time-management and boundary issues. Fueling my nonstop pace were some deeply rooted and very distorted ideas about God, myself, and the how and why of life with God. My hope is that in the pages that follow I'll be able to pass on to you some of the healing insights that restored my soul and gave me a profound sense of coming home to myself—and an intimacy with God that I'd always wanted.

———

For most of my life, I have been overwhelmed by the distractions of busyness, noise, and hurry. Now I know that God did not design my life to run on empty.

—POINTS TO PONDER—

1. How have distractions such as noise, demands, and frenzied schedules impacted your life? Have these pressures ever brought you to a crisis point in your health and/or in your life of faith? If so, what was the outcome?

2. What words most accurately describe the rhythm of your life? Do these words fall more into the category of "balanced, peaceful, and centered" or into the realm of "pressured, fatigued, and out of control"? If you feel changes are needed, what first step can you take this week toward positive change?

3. What are the things in life that your heart is most set on? How closely do these things align with becoming the person God made you to be?

A WORLD STUCK ON FAST FORWARD

Working Longer and Harder Doesn't Work

We've learned how to make a living, but not a life;
we've added years to life, not life to years.
We've cleaned up the air, but polluted the soul.
We've split the atom, but not our prejudice.
We plan more, but accomplish less.
We've learned to rush, but not to wait.
These are days of quick trips, disposable diapers,
throw-away morality, one-night stands, overweight bodies,
and pills that do everything from cheer, to quiet, to kill.
It is a time when there is much in the show window
and nothing in the stockroom.

—UNKNOWN

Just getting through a typical day often feels like I'm making my way along a busy thoroughfare, both sides of the road crowded with large, brightly colored billboards. Each word on each billboard shouts for my attention: "Buy me, hire me, drive me, taste me, drink me, wear me." And above all, they shout, "Notice me!"

Not only is our society constantly trying to sell us products and services, it also sells misleading ideas about security, success, and comfort. If we're not watchful, those misleading sales pitches will deform our lives. Advertising is the loudest voice in our era, bent on reshaping us to conform to its image.

Short of moving into a remote cabin in the mountains, we can't escape the reach of advertising. Closed-circuit television brings product advertising into schools. Pop-up ads assault us on the Internet. Display ads in airports cater to our materialism. Prominently displayed brand-name logos at concerts and sports events saturate us with brand identity. Infomercials made to look like documentaries or talk shows push an astounding variety of products that people don't need. But the "beauty" of all this is that you no longer have to drive to the store. You can easily order an item you don't need without leaving your home.

The early fathers and mothers of the church considered society, in their own day, to be a shipwreck from which any sane person must swim for his or her life. These holy women and men believed that if Christians simply drifted along, passively allowing the beliefs and values of the world to influence them, it would certainly lead to their complete demise.[1] Centuries later I know exactly what they meant. The apostle Paul had his own way of saying it: "Don't become so well-adjusted to your culture that you fit into it without even thinking" (Romans 12:2, MSG).

The damaging effect of living in a society filled with values and stresses and temptations about achievement, security, and contentment is enormous. Author Dallas Willard describes a scientific experiment that compared stress levels between a solitary laboratory mouse and a group of mice penned up in close quarters. Researchers found that it took a higher dose of amphetamines to kill a mouse living in solitude. The reason? Even though a much smaller dose was administered to the mice in a group, they begin hopping around and hyping each other up. With the frenzy created in the group, a dosage *twenty times smaller* proved to be deadly. The most remarkable finding was that a mouse that had been given *no* amphetamines, after being placed in a group of mice that were on the drug, became so hyperactive that in ten minutes it was dead.[2]

You and I are not mice, of course. We are created in God's image. But when it comes to the way our culture affects us, we bear remarkable similarity to ordinary lab animals. If we allow our lives to be reshaped by the world around us, we will certainly suffer a deadly outcome.

Last year in South Carolina the news reported that a man's pet cobra had bitten his son, and the local hospital did not have the necessary antivenin to counteract the snake's deadly poison. Fortunately, the boy was airlifted to a hospital in Florida where antivenin was administered. Before the injection was given, the boy had already become paralyzed and suffered from a dangerously high fever. If the deadly threat of the world's influence were as immediate as cobra venom, we'd take it more seriously. Our lives are in jeopardy, but it's easy to ignore the danger since the deadly effects are gradual. We barely acknowledge the constant sales pitches, but they are no less destructive. Take, for example, the pervasive marketing of busyness.

Loving the Murderer

If you live in North America, you are a prime candidate for slow death by overstimulation. Your environment is busy depleting you with noise, distractions, and the compulsion to always be in a hurry. If I had set out to destroy my identity as a beloved child of God, I couldn't have done better than living in America at the start of the twenty-first century. The greatest threats I've encountered are not the arguments of skeptics or the lure of drink, drugs, or sex. The greatest threats are the constant busyness and frantic hurry that demand my allegiance. Author Robert Benson says, "We take our place in the race and watch our lives disappear in the daily grind."[3] We rarely are grounded in the present moment (where God is to be encountered) because we're always rushing out beyond it or replaying in our minds our disappointing past. Shame and sadness over our dark past drives us to strive for a brighter future, which generally winds up being busier rather than better.

I'm as vulnerable as a recovering alcoholic working in a liquor store. I've begun many days with a fresh resolve to resist the lure of busyness only to discover I'm not as strong as I thought I was. I can easily convince myself that amid the noise and bustle I'll still hear the voice of God and accomplish all I long to do. Like a sober alcoholic eying the poison of a fifth of whiskey, only later am I forced to face the deadly reality. The noise, busyness, and hurry deliver nothing but a heart that's hard of hearing and a life of anxious longing and weary disappointment. The poison is gradual but still terminal.

I recall Edmund's encounter with Jadis, the White Witch in *The Lion, the Witch, and the Wardrobe.* Jadis easily seduced the boy with Turkish Delight. The more he ate, the more he wanted to eat. Of course, Edmund didn't realize that this was enchanted Turkish Delight and that those who once tasted it "would want more and more of it, and would even, if they were allowed, go on eating it till they killed themselves."[4] "The press of busyness is like a charm," said Søren Kierkegaard. "Its power swells...it reaches out seeking always to lay hold of ever younger victims so that childhood or youth are scarcely allowed the quiet and the retirement in which the Eternal may unfold a divine growth."[5]

The crazy truth is that as much as we complain about it, we actually *want* to be seduced by busyness. But why do we love the killer? In part, it's because when we're busy, we don't have to think about important matters we prefer to avoid. Busyness enables us to quiet the voice of the deeper issues that trouble and haunt us. Plus busyness makes us feel important. Everyone prefers action and adventure to boredom.

Sadly, like eating enchanted Turkish Delight, if we don't stop, we will go on with our busyness until it kills us.

LOSING THE SIMPLE RHYTHMS

There are times I'm sick of heart. It's similar to the sadness you feel when you're leaving on yet another business trip, knowing you'll miss your son's big game. For me the sadness comes as I call to mind the rhythm of my life when I was younger—back when life seemed so much lighter. I miss the times when the world seemed to stop, take a deep breath, and rest. Sundays were like that when I was a boy. If you found that you were out of bread or milk, it was hard to find a store that was open where you could buy even a few essentials. I remember holidays, too, when all businesses closed so their employees and customers could enjoy a much-needed day of celebration and rest. This was long before the days of twenty-four-hour superstores. Living now in a world that never seems to stop for rest, much less slow down, raises my anxiety level. I feel as if I've left something undone. I've lost the rhythm of work and rest that God designed in our world and into our very being.

I once asked my father-in-law about his life when he was a young boy, growing up on a farm in South Carolina. "Do you remember life being as noisy, busy, and hurried as it is today?" I asked. Looking at me with an incredulous smile, he responded, "Don't go thinking that noise and being busy and hurried are newfangled inventions. I remember getting up with the sun and working hard all day long. But when the sun went down, we knew how to call it quits!" After a thoughtful pause he added, "Some of my most favorite memories are of our family lounging on the front porch or playing in the yard on a warm summer night or sitting in front of the fire on cold evenings."

Men and women back then were no strangers to hard work. But they were wise enough to live in balance. When did we stop calling it quits at the end of the day? And a better question, *Why?*

Several decades ago futurists predicted the arrival of the "leisure society," a world that would demand less work. Testimony before

Senate subcommittees in the 1960s forecast that new technology would speed up the work process so much that people would soon be dealing with the "problem" of extra free time. Americans would wonder what to do with all their newfound freedom. Sadly, the futurists were wrong. Greater efficiency has pushed us to use our time for more productivity and more work. Instead of becoming the leisure society, we've become the most driven, most stressed-out society in history.

Juliet Schor's book *The Overworked American* was a bestseller, although I suspect very few had time to read it. The United States now leads Japan as the longest-working nation in the advanced industrial world. It's interesting to note that if you are German and you work more than thirty-seven hours a week and take fewer than five weeks of vacation per year, you're considered a workaholic. Ours is the most vacation-starved country in the world.[6]

I don't want to overlook the benefits of modern technology. If your car breaks down late at night, it's great to be able to call a tow truck on your cell phone. But while the so-called labor-saving devices have made many tasks easier, they've also led us to work longer hours and to cram more into our lives. I remember the first time my brother Steve was interrupted on the golf course by the ringing of his phone. I'm sure he's not the last to use that as an excuse for a poor drive! Another friend spent the first three days of his family vacation setting up his computer to follow stock quotations. Once he got his contraption set up and forced his twenty-four-hundred-baud modem to dial long distance, it took forever to receive the tiny red and green numbers. Who do you think missed him more—those share prices or his wife and children?

Reflecting on the stories of frustration, loneliness, and disappointment I've heard from highly successful people, I wonder, *Will we ever see that our social and economic gains often come at the expense of the things we long for most?* Echoing in my mind are the words of Jesus, "For what will it profit them if they gain the whole world but forfeit their life? Or what will they give in return for their life?" (Matthew 16:26).

Syndicated columnist William Safire offered an unsettling appraisal of our obsession with work and always being busy, as evidenced by our efforts to be constantly available. To illustrate, he referred to the late actress Greta Garbo, who played the part of a depressed ballerina in the 1932 movie *Grand Hotel.* Upon discovering a jewel thief in her hotel room, she delivered what became her signature line: "I vant to be alone."[7]

Along with Safire, I share Garbo's desire for privacy. With pagers and cell phones, faxes and instant messaging, e-mail and voice mail, streaming audio and video, the world is simply too much with us. In my lust to be in constant communication, I've squandered away my long-held value of personal freedom.

When I left my position with Young Life, I was fortunate to have three months off before beginning my next career. I anticipated the freedom I'd have to spend my days alone with God. Looking back, however, I recall spending very little time in God's company. Examining how I used three months of free time caused me to ask some difficult questions: Do I really want to live every moment in God's presence? Do I long for God, craving his company? Have I determined to be his, and *only* his, for all of my days?

The problem was not a lack of time; it was my lack of joyful, enthusiastic delight in God, my lack of deep affection directed toward him at every hour of the day. It seems to be a fact of life that when we're left with a choice, we choose to do the things that matter to us most.

So what mattered to me the most? For one, I needed to be in constant contact with others. I felt that if I wasn't available, others would forget I existed, or worse, they'd begin thinking that I didn't matter. Feeding this fear was the fundamental belief that I had no real worth apart from the things I accomplished when I was busy. Wanting to be busy and constantly available to others grew out of the feeling that if I were ever left alone, I'd disappear. Spending time alone with God didn't seem to *accomplish* anything other than to feed the fear that I'd be forgotten.

A couple of summers ago a story circulated around Wrightsville Beach about an investment banker from a large city who was vacationing in this delightful North Carolina coastal town. Standing on a small pier late one afternoon, he watched as a lone fisherman docked his small boat. Inside the boat were several large yellowtail tuna.

The banker complimented the fisherman on the quality of his fish and asked how long it took to catch them.

The local replied, "Only a little while."

The banker then asked, "Why didn't you stay out longer and catch more fish?"

The local said, "With this I have more than enough to feed my family and share some with my friends."

The banker then asked, "But what do you do with the rest of your time?"

The fisherman said, "I sleep late, fish a little, play with my children, take naps with my wife, stroll into town each evening where I sip wine and play the guitar with my friends. I have a full and busy life."

The banker scoffed, "I could help you. You should spend more time fishing and with the proceeds buy a bigger boat. Then with the proceeds from the bigger boat, you could buy several boats. Eventually you would have a fleet of fishing boats. Instead of selling your catch to a middleman, you would sell directly to the processor, eventually opening your own cannery. You would control the product, processing, and distribution. You would, however, have to move to a larger city, perhaps eventually to New York where you would run your ever-expanding enterprise."

The fisherman, intrigued, asked, "But how long will all this take?"

"Fifteen to twenty years," the banker replied.

"But what then?" asked the fisherman.

The banker laughed. "Here's the best part. When the time is right you would announce an IPO and sell your company stock to the public and become very rich. You would make millions."

"Millions?" the fisherman asked. "Then what?"

The banker said, "Then you would retire, move to a small fishing town where you would sleep late, play with your kids, take naps with your wife, stroll into town in the evenings where you would sip wine and play your guitar with your friends."

SPREADING THE DISEASE

When I started working with adolescents in the early 1970s, I maintained a list of the students I saw regularly. The list included their name, mailing address, and home phone number. Today I have a similar list of the teenagers and adults I contact regularly. However, there's a disturbingly noticeable difference. In addition to their name, mailing address, and home phone number is their e-mail address, instant messenger screen name, mobile number, pager number, and work number. Some even have their own Web sites. It's unsettling to see how they've learned to be so busy and always available!

My heart grows particularly sad when I think about the pressure adolescents live under. I wonder what part I might have played in spreading this dreadful disease. Many of the adolescents I know are asking what happened to their free time. Some never had any to start with. Between music lessons, tutoring, sports practices, school club meetings, and part-time jobs, they somehow manage to fit homework in. And those who also are involved in church youth groups or Christian clubs have even more commitments to juggle. Unless free time gets scheduled into a calendar or PDA, it just doesn't happen. There's something awe-inspiring, and at the same time sad, seeing my high school friends open up their Day-Timers.

When I ask them about the pace of the world they've been thrust into, none seem particularly grateful to have been born in this age. They don't enjoy having every minute crammed with productivity. They're alert to the things that distract their parents, things like cell phones at soccer games, laptops on vacations, and voice mail on weekends, and it bothers them that anything could be more important to Mom or Dad than they are. My thirteen-year-old son, Lee, got in the car with me and found me on the phone. When I later asked him what he felt, he said, "Disappointed."

I've heard other adolescents express anger, frustration, and disappointment over their parents and with the mind-boggling pace of their own lives. They want to know why no one takes time just to chill and relax.

Living in this pressure-cooker environment, kids have become multitaskers, juggling half a dozen activities without missing a beat. One ten-year-old I know had one hundred names in her Buddy List before her parents gave both their daughter—and her computer—a rest. She was capable of handling ten or so chat sessions simultaneously, one for each year of her life. There seems to be no limit to the number of things even preadolescents juggle. However, there is ample reason to be concerned about the effects of multitasking on a young person's ability to focus. Someone said, "To do two things at once is to do neither."

The term *data smog* describes the atmosphere teenagers live in. Multitasking is fun and accomplishment does matter, but I'm afraid we're raising a generation of kids who could become so addicted to the buzz of multitasking that as they mature, they'll lose some of the values they (and we) hold dear, values like patience and tranquillity. And in the end, restlessness will be their sad reward.

Kids spend more time in a myriad of after-school activities and less time riding bikes aimlessly in their neighborhood, more hours on the practice field and fewer moments of dinner-table conversation. I began asking people about the frequency of their shared meals. Many seemed alarmed when they stopped to ponder their answer. When I probed for answers concerning how intimate and personal the conversations around the table typically are and how often they would linger at the table after a meal, hardly any gave an encouraging answer.

Not only are the lives of most adults out of control; we've passed this deadly virus on to the next generation. Psychologist Carl Jung years ago said, "Busyness is not *of* the devil, busyness *is* the devil."[8] Busyness by itself doesn't threaten to kill me. What threatens to kill me is how easily I assign undeserved meaning to the many things I'm busy doing.

WHY THE DEATH WISH?

The questions are simple: Why am I prone to live this way? Why do I work so long and so hard? Why am I so driven and so preoccupied? What would make me want to rest less than God rests? The "disconnect" between what I *want* and what I *do* is huge. Yet when I look at the hectic, pressured, and exhausting world we live in, how could the disconnect be anything but huge?

Certainly part of the problem is that companies are staffing with fewer employees while demanding increased production. Productivity increases as each employee produces more, which typically translates into longer hours, fewer vacation days, and taking work home. We complain about the work load but quickly add that we're afraid to work less for fear of losing our jobs. The United States has the most productive work force in the world; therefore, part of the problem is corporate America, not just internal forces such as insecurity or a misdirected sense of identity.

Years ago Barbara Walters interviewed media mogul Ted Turner. At the end of their conversation, she recounted many of Turner's accomplishments: his ownership of a Major League Baseball team and several television networks, his prowess as a sailor, and his tremendous wealth. Then after a long pause, just moments before the interview ended, she asked her final question: "What does it feel like to be so wealthy?" Turner responded, "It's like a paper bag. Everyone sees the bag. Everyone wants it. Once you get the bag, you discover that the bag is empty."[9] In a rare, unrehearsed moment, Turner seemed to be saying his life might be full but still unfulfilled.

But what about the church? Isn't it the one place where noise, hurry, and the frantic pace of life diminish? Quite the contrary. The busy, noisy church has become the norm. In addition to the regular demands and usual pressures of jobs and families, the church and all it encompasses must be served as well. The badly needed programs of most churches present endless demands. And tragically, many pastors are functioning workaholics. The example of their life calls others to be, if not all things to all people, at least a lot more of everything than most people feel capable of being. Many of the successful vocational ministers I've known are busy succeeding because of what's lacking on the inside. They seek greater external success to try to fill an empty internal well that was drained of joy by their loss of connection with God. I lived that same life for years. The busy, noisy, and hurried environment inherent in most churches raises expectations to an unrealistic, inhumane level.

A few years ago, while visiting a widely known and highly regarded pastor, I spoke candidly of my belief that a solid foundation for a person's life and service can be built only upon a deep and intimate relationship with God. As he listened, his expression grew somber. "The people in my church are literally dying from their lack of this kind of foundation...and so is their pastor."

It's a simple thing to identify the fundamental cause of the weakening of personal spirituality among clergy and parachurch workers. Most spend frighteningly little time cultivating their personal relationship with God, and many have no one to talk with about their interior life. A staggering number have indicated they don't have a close friend.

I believe the same dynamic is at work in the lives of parishioners. The overload seems to express itself in a simple pattern: overscheduled at work, underscheduled at home, and unscheduled when it comes to nourishing one's soul. Exactly what I often discover in my own life.

Whose World Am I Living In?

We can learn life-changing lessons from paying attention to the lives of others. Seeing the foolish mistakes of another on the big screen of life invites me, if I'm honest, to recognize and admit my own missteps and failures.

The lyrics and melody of the hymn "This Is My Father's World" have been, for me, a source of reassurance and encouragement. More than anything, my heart yearns for the intimacy with God that is expressed here. But it has been equally significant to observe the life of the hymnwriter Maltbie Babcock.

The sixteen-stanza poem, written in the spirit of many of the Old Testament psalms, contains these soothing lines:

This is my Father's world, and to my listening ears,
All nature sings, and round me rings the music of the spheres.
This is my Father's world: I rest me in the thought.[10]

I can't read these words without hearing their powerful, positive melody. Had Babcock continued to nurture a life of congruence with his lyrics, it's likely he would have lived longer than forty-three years. A highly talented and successful athlete, musician, actor, and student, Babcock was a deeply spiritual man. After graduating from Auburn Theological Seminary, he was ordained as a Presbyterian minister and began his first pastorate in Lockport, New York, a small but beautiful town on the banks of the Erie Canal.

During the first years of his pastorate he would go out early in the morning or late at night to the brow of a hill some two miles north of the city to take in the beauty of nature and commune with God. Viewing Lake Ontario in the distance or wandering through a nearby forest, he found refuge from life's pressures. I can still recall being fresh out of college and making time to be still for similar times of reflection. Lucky man, this Maltbie Babcock, near so much wind and water, hill and vale, sunlit days and starry nights.

His experiences in nature must have inspired him to write:

This is my Father's world, the birds their carols raise;
The morning light, the lily white declare their Maker's praise.
This is my Father's world: He shines in all that's fair;
In the rustling grass I hear Him pass;
He speaks to me everywhere.[11]

Babcock's life soon took a different path. The leisurely walks and intimate communion with nature and God were soon forsaken. Who knows, maybe his congregation figured he didn't have enough to do, and so they beckoned him to start earlier, stay later, and chair more committees. "Don't just walk in the woods, do something!" And then, when the invitation from a prominent church in Baltimore came (Babcock must have had a fondness for big water), this talented young servant, not yet thirty years of age, left Lockport to assume his new and more demanding responsibilities. But not before he penned the words:

This is my Father's world. Oh let me ne'er forget
That though the wrong seems oft so strong, God is the
    ruler yet.[12]

The road he traveled has an eerie familiarity. For the next fourteen years Babcock offered effective and, no doubt, tireless service, not only to his church but also to the students of Johns Hopkins University and the city of Baltimore at large. Vast numbers of individuals were spiritually nurtured by his contagiously radiant personality.

In 1899, at the age of forty-one, he was invited to succeed the highly regarded Henry van Dyke at the much larger Brick Presbyterian Church in New York City. Although the decision was difficult, Babcock felt compelled to accept the opportunity. Sadly, in his new setting he found less time for nurturing his soul at the very point in his life when he needed it the most. The demands and pressures continued taking their toll. While he did his best to seize every opportunity to get away and commune with God, those opportunities became fewer and farther between. Reflecting on his demanding life, he picked up the pen again and wrote a poem that appears to reflect a shift in his focus, from living in the peace that comes with knowing you are loved by God to something far less comforting. Here are his autobiographical lines:

Be strong!
We are not here to play, to dream, to drift;
We have hard work to do and loads to lift;
Shun not the struggle, face it, 'tis God's gift.
Be strong, be strong, be strong![13]

Finally, after just eighteen months in New York, the people of his congregation sent Babcock on a trip to the Holy Land with the hope that he would be able to recuperate from the toll his service to others had taken. On the trip, at the age of forty-three and at the pinnacle of his influence and power, Maltbie Babcock met an untimely death, some believe from brucellosis.[14]

As I contemplate his premature death, I can't help but feel gratitude for the grace of God that interrupted my life and set me on a different course years ago when a spiritual director asked me to tell him about the condition of my soul. What do you think happened to Maltbie Babcock between "All nature sings, and round me rings the music of the spheres" and "Be strong! / We are not here to play, to dream, to drift; / We have hard work to do and loads to lift"? Was it his feeling compelled to be productive for God that did him in, or was it his loss of discernment about when to work and when to rest that brought his early demise?

———

I've always heard that it takes a crook to catch a crook, and Maltbie Babcock's choice to be strong and lift heavy loads (and, sadly, to die young) sounds all too familiar. In his kindness and mercy, God has shown me that I am here to *play,* to *dream,* and to *drift* as much as to do the hard work I've been given. I believe God recognizes there's holiness to my play that's as sacred and real as the holiness of my prayer. I believe God knows that without playing there will eventually be no praying. God knows the constant noise, endless activity, and dreadfully hurried pace that permeate our culture will misdirect your life and mine, just as placing a compass near a magnet will draw the needle away from true north.

In the next chapter we'll look at our understanding of God's nature and character and how our view of God determines the way we choose to live. You might be in for the most welcome surprise of your life.

—POINTS TO PONDER—

1. In what ways have you "become so well-adjusted to your culture that you fit into it without even thinking" (see

Romans 12:2, MSG)? How has the pace of your life hindered your relationships with others?

2. Do you believe your life is in step with how God intends for you to live? If not, in what ways does your life depart from God's desires for you?

3. Is there any sacred playing, dreaming, and drifting in your life right now? If not, how can you begin to carve out time to play, dream, and drift?

3

A CONDESCENDING
VIEW OF GOD

The Straight Path to Soul Starvation

*What comes into our minds when we think about God
is the most important thing about us.*

—A. W. Tozer, *Knowledge of the Holy*

Like every child, I was taught that "sticks and stones may break
my bones, but words will never hurt me." And just like you, I
know that it's a lie.

In an earlier chapter I told the story of my emotional and spiritual
exhaustion during my junior year of college. I experienced much-
needed healing during two weeks spent in a hospital psychiatric ward.
Then, just a few days after my release, my fiancée's family invited me
to their home for dinner. Given the circumstances, I expected a quiet
evening together celebrating the first completed lap on my road to
recovery.

So much for expectations. I sensed from the strained dinner conversation that trouble was lurking. While we ate dessert, my hereto-
fore future mother-in-law blindsided me with a question: "Fil, are you
emotionally equipped for marriage, or are you, as we suspect, too
weak?" To be truthful, I'm not sure what I told her. However, I'm certain it wasn't the answer she was hoping for. The following day my

fiancée called to announce that she was breaking our engagement. "I can't marry a weak man" was the only explanation she gave.

Her assessment of me as a weak man was more devastating than the thought of knowing we'd never marry each other. I would gladly have suffered a physical attack—bring on the sticks and stones—in place of her verbal assault.

The English language, so I've heard, contains more than four hundred thousand unique words, most of which mean the same to me as they do for everybody else. However, certain words mean something totally different to me than they do to others. My response to a written or spoken word depends on the actual word, my associations with that word, and to some extent my imagination. Of course, as I process a word spoken by another, my mind is filling in the blanks, providing a definition that may or may not be accurate. If as a child you were accused of being a crybaby, then when a friend says you're an emotional person, you might read too much into what she is saying. The friend simply means that you feel things deeply, a trait she may very well admire. But you think she is accusing you of being unstable or irrational.

Although words appear as mere marks on paper, pixels on a screen, or sounds that fill the air, some words have power enough to control me. One little word or a string of words holds enough power to make me laugh or cry, love or despise, fight or flee. Certain words, if arranged in a particular order or spoken with a certain inflection, can change my mood and even change my mind. The power of words amazes me!

It's All in the Name

Particularly fascinating is how we use words to identify one being from another. This extends from our children and our friends to identifying our pets, each with a unique name. Imagine how confusing it would be if, at chowtime, every dog were called Fido. And names go far beyond simply reducing the chance for confusion. A person's name holds power. When Lucie and I were trying to decide what we would name each of our children, we based our decision in part on the feeling that we associated with that particular name. More than once we said, "We could never call a child by *that* name!" (Remember hymnwriter Maltbie Babcock from chapter 2? What were *his* parents thinking?)

The most powerful word, or name, is *God.* When my thinking about God is correct, consistent, and focused, I am, in some way, thinking correctly about everything else. When my thinking about God is incorrect, inconsistent, or disjointed, I am thinking incorrectly about everything else in my life. More than anything else, I need a right view of God.

I'm convinced that my need for constant activity is deeply rooted in terribly flawed images of God, images of my own making. The root cause of my busyness might be explained this way: My default nature is set to believe that God's acceptance, love, and care for me is directly proportional to my level of activity for God. This belief system—the more I do for God, the more God will love me—has dictated my every waking activity more than anything else. And it has threatened to starve my soul.

Looking back over the flow of my life, I see where I've been mistaken about most *everything* at one time or another. I've been wrong about whether someone is trustworthy or a scoundrel, whether my shoes go with my slacks, and whether a certain movie is worth our time and money. Yet when I think back on my most costly mistakes, I realize they rested squarely on my frequent misconceptions of God.

Voltaire said, "If God created us in his own image we have more than reciprocated."[1] My reconstituted versions of God were not a compliment, rather they were disappointments to the God I love. I would even go so far as to say that my reconstituted versions of God were the leading causes of my frustration, loneliness, disappointment, and shame…and, you guessed it, my busyness. My beliefs about God say more about me than about him. Ignorance of this truth holds me captive, leaving me with an impotent god of my own making. And for most of my life I've let this lesser god subject me to its haunts, hurts, and demands. The god of my own making is a cruel taskmaster.

If I could champion one cause, it would be to proclaim that nothing warps our souls so badly as a condescending view of God. Looking back, I can see myself growing up with an image of a god whose favorite hobby was being mad at me. In fact, he was angry with me most all the time. I grew up in the buckle of the Bible Belt, where the portrait of an angry God was painted vividly in many ways and places. The misinformation came mainly from family, friends, and church. I was troubled by this harsh image, but it appeared that many of my friends and family members were happy with an angry God. If others had come to terms with this harsh God, then I could find a way.

I concluded that the best way to respond to an angry God was to earn his acceptance. I paid a high price with the currency of good behavior. God's acceptance was directly proportional to my maintaining a set of rules. By the age of twelve I had "learned" that things like memorizing Scripture verses, not thinking evil thoughts, and "acting Christian" gained me more of God's favor. In addition were the obligatory Sunday school classes, worship services, Vacation Bible Schools, and abstinence from many forms of entertainment. You know the standard taboos: no movies, no card playing, no dancing, no swimming with girls, no baseball on Sunday. I could live without poker and dancing, but I was never allowed to go to a movie or play baseball on Sunday. That hurt.

Not only did God want all my time, God also wanted all my energy. Ignorant of the full truth of God's grace, my feelings became my only yardstick for measuring success or failure. The more miserable I felt, the yardstick said, the better I must be doing for God. I hated Sunday school more than any regularly scheduled activity on my calendar in junior and senior high school, yet nothing would excuse me from ever being at church on Sunday. Naturally, this nurtured the misconception that what's important to God is outward behavior, not what's in one's heart.

I grew up disliking God, or at least the intractable god that I was taught to obey. What was there to like? Sure, I *loved* God (I was afraid *not* to), but I didn't *like* God. Is there anything likable about an all-powerful parent who is constantly harsh and demanding?

Encounters with a Self-Made God

I had my first dramatic encounter with the god of my own making in grammar school. I remember "committing my life" to him, which is how they referred to a conversion experience at my church. In responding to the appeal of a visiting speaker, I walked the aisle to lay my life on the altar. I knew from then on that the sincerity of my decision would be gauged in how well I did (or didn't) in controlling, among other things, my speech. Not many days later I was playing basketball with friends when I uttered a clearly out-of-bounds word. Time stood still for a moment, and then I ran off the court with tears streaming from my eyes. *I've blown it! What a miserable disappointment I am to God. Surely my relationship with him is over!* The hurt and shame of that experience are still fresh. Soon enough I was back on track, vowing never to curse again. Those more mature in these matters assured me that God could forgive this careless setback and that, if I were wise, I would see this as a lesson to be learned—one that, if I tried hard enough, wouldn't have to be repeated. Again, outward appearances were elevated above the spiritual condition of my heart.

By high school the focus on outward appearances took the form of an insatiable craving for acceptance. I would do anything to gain the approval of the crowd. Actually, *crowds.* I had two sets of friends, for whom I adopted two different standards of behavior. With my "godless" friends, I appeared godless, and with my "faith-full friends," I appeared faith-full. It was a difficult balancing act, but like anyone who gets rewarded, I learned quickly.

I have countless memories of summer days with church friends, going to the beach to do towel-to-towel evangelism. When evening came, I'd return to the beach with my other friends. We'd drink beer, try to pick up girls, and vandalize nearby property. With both groups of friends, I desperately longed for approval.

In the process of living this way, I came to think of God as someone I controlled. I could make God angry, sad, or happy simply by choosing how to act. If I did enough good things, God was happy. If I fouled up enough, God was angry. It seemed that I could finally control my life and, in the process, control God.

My image of a controllable God was deeply rooted in an accepted belief system of that time. At church we were told regularly how badly God needed our help. The God I grew up with was terribly anemic. If there were to be any hope for the world, this God must receive a major transfusion in the form of more workers. Always he needed more help than he was getting.

I remember the first time I walked down the aisle of our Baptist church in response to a plea for people to go to foreign lands as missionaries. I was in high school. I recall thinking, *If the need is so great that God could use me, then I had better get going!* Refusing to volunteer my services would have been as heartless as driving past an elderly woman stranded on the side of the road with a flat tire. In this case, God was stranded and needed my help. Back then my life was driven by the pressure to do *something.* So I was constantly doing things without much thought to the deeper meaning of the life of faith.

Religious Compulsions

You might think that after high school and college, I'd grow up and recognize God for who God really is. Maybe as an adult, I'd accept God on God's terms. Think again.

After graduating from college, I joined the staff of Young Life. For the first fifteen years I devoted myself daily to trying to build friendships with high school folks who were, for the most part, disinterested in God. I wanted to help them realize that their lack of interest in God stemmed from their misconceptions of God. Often I'd say, "If I believed the things about God that you do, I wouldn't be interested either." I thought my own thinking about God was correct while they were sadly mistaken. I failed to realize that I, too, was badly misguided. Their misconceptions led them to reject God while mine were driving me to please and impress God. We were all wrong.

A scene from the 1999 movie *The Big Kahuna* reminds me of a season in my life I wish hadn't occurred. Kevin Spacey and Danny DeVito play two businessmen who are loyal and trusting friends. Late one night the two friends are sitting in the shadows of a dimly lit hotel suite. Phil, DeVito's character, begins reminiscing about a dream he once had as a child.

"I found God hiding in a closet in the middle of a burnt-out city. The city was destroyed by fire or some kind of explosion. And there in the middle of it was a coat closet, standing there all by itself. I walked up to the closet and opened the door. Inside, God was hiding. I remember he had a big lion head. But I knew he wasn't a lion. It was God. And he was afraid.... And I reached out my hand to lead him out of the closet and said to him: 'Don't be afraid God, I'm on your side.' And we stood there, the two of us holding hands looking out over the destruction."[2]

I wept during this scene. A friend says we should pay close attention to the things that make us cry, for there we are not far from the heart of God or our own. Author Frederick Buechner advises, "Whenever you find tears in your eyes, especially unexpected tears, it is well to pay the closest attention. They are not only telling you something about the secret of who you are, but more often than not God is speaking to you through them of the mystery of where you have come from and is summoning you to where, if your soul is to be saved, you should go next."[3] I backed up the tape and replayed the scene a number of times, looking for what had prompted my tears. Then it hit me. This was my picture of God from years ago. This was me, living in the illusion that God was in desperate trouble and that in all my frenzied activity I was somehow coming to God's rescue. Back in those days, without knowing it, I was clinging to the hope that if I did enough for God, then God just might begin to like me. If I helped God enough, he might appreciate me enough to be friends with me.

My ceaseless activity for God was the driving force in my life. That late night in front of rewinding videotape, God opened up the scrapbook of my earlier life. I wept, seeing glimpses of my mistaken images of God. Later, when I began to discover how to think correctly about God, I knew that while I was weeping over my unredeemed life, God was weeping with joy for the child of God I was becoming.

Being misunderstood is a terrible thing, and who knows more about being misunderstood than God?

Having It All Wrong

I had become an out-of-control work addict, what author and educator Parker Palmer calls a "functional atheist."[4] Although I spoke of God as being powerful and in control, my actions told a different story, that God either didn't exist or was seriously ill. I lived in the illusion that unless I was making it happen, nothing was happening. Not only was my life shaped by an incorrect view of a too-small God, an equally incorrect view of a too-big me made matters worse. Once firmly planted, my mistaken views made arrogance second nature... and my life dangerously active.

I elevated my self-importance and diminished God's to the extent that even the act of coming to God was something I took credit for, speaking of "my" decision to follow God, as if Jesus were some innocent bystander with no part to play in the drama of my life. I had ignored Jesus' words, "No one can come to me unless drawn by the Father who sent me" (John 6:44).

Overlooking God's initiative in pursuing me was a mistake that began to take its toll. It is reported that Martin Luther once said, "While I drink my little glass of Wittenberg beer, the gospel runs its course."[5] Surely this is one of the truest and most reassuring things ever said about beer and God in the same breath. Our relationship with God is not the result of our efforts. Rather, a loving and gracious God acted on our behalf, granting us a most benevolent gift.

Coming to see that God has searched me out and found me—and not the other way around—was breathtaking. I was beginning to understand that my faith in God is oftentimes greater when I rest than when I am busy. For a compulsive overachiever, this was a revolutionary thought. The truth that God could love me just as I was, without my doing a thing for him, seemed too good to be true.

GETTING A CLEAR PICTURE

We can't gain a right view of God without a core focus and dependence on Jesus. Of him, the apostle Paul wrote, "Now Christ is the visible expression of the invisible God" (Colossians 1:15, Phillips). In other words, Jesus Christ is the best snapshot God has ever had taken of himself. If I earnestly wish to know and understand the character and nature of God, I can't do better than to carefully observe the person of Jesus Christ. However, the question remained. How would I get a clear picture of Jesus' personality and character? How would I ever really know what was in his heart?

In an effort to make clear the mystery, the apostle John wrote, "The Word became flesh and blood, and moved into the neighborhood. We saw the glory with our own eyes, the one-of-a-kind glory, like Father, like Son, generous inside and out, true from start to finish" (John 1:14, MSG). Jesus Christ is the eternal Word who became fully human and lived on earth as you and I do. He is the personal disclosure of God, the most phenomenal wonder and mystery in all of human history. Jesus Christ was born into the world and became completely God and completely man. The amazing thing is that this act of utter humility continues even today as Jesus Christ becomes flesh again and again through the words of sacred Scripture. Jesus Christ can be encountered in a dynamic way today through words that are "living and active, sharper than any two-edged sword" (Hebrews 4:12).

My life was saved from the killing power of busyness by coming to really know God through Jesus. Knowing Jesus has saved others from my hurtful ways and saved me from self-destruction.

Nothing has been more effective in slowing the relentless pace of my driven life than this clearer picture of God found in Jesus. As I've gained a more accurate understanding of God's character and nature and what lies within God's heart, I've been granted a more solid character, a more peaceful nature, and a quieter, more tender, more teachable heart. I'm discovering that Jesus Christ is God's perfect response to every longing in my heart. In part 2 of this book we'll look closely at some of the resources God makes available to help us clarify and deepen our understanding of who God is.

The very essence of God's nature is compassion, and the counsel of sacred Scripture suggests that the words *tender* and *sensitive* most accurately describe God's disposition toward us. Nothing I am capable of doing will ever cause God to love me more, simply because

God can't love me any more. And nothing I ever do will cause God to love me less; God can't do that either. That idea used to sound like madness to me. Then I realized that, in a way, it *is* madness. It makes no rational sense that God would love me this way! As someone said, "God is drunk with love for me." The love of God is a divine choice that can't be comprehended or explained in human terms.

Finding words to describe this divine "madness" is an endless challenge. Years ago a powerful African American speaker, Dr. Samuel M. Lockeridge, preached a sermon with more eloquence, passion, and clarity than I'd ever witnessed. He painted the most profoundly clear word picture of Jesus I've heard. I was reintroduced to his message in Anne Graham Lotz's book *Just Give Me Jesus,* and I often return to his expressions, especially whenever I feel I'm getting off course. The wisdom and power of Lockeridge's words have proven a helpful aid in keeping my pace saner.

He is enduringly strong.
  He is entirely sincere.
He is eternally steadfast.
  He is immortally gracious.
He's imperially powerful.
  He's impartially merciful.
He is the greatest phenomenon that has ever crossed
    the horizons of the globe.

He is God's Son.
  He is the sinner's Savior.
He is the captive's Ransom.
  He is the Breath of Life.
He is the centerpiece of civilization.
  He stands in the solitude of Himself.

He is august and He is unique.

    He is unparalleled and He is unprecedented.

He is undisputed and He is undefiled.

    He is unsurpassed and He is unshakable.

He is the loftiest idea in philosophy.

    He is the highest personality in psychology.

He is the supreme subject in literature.

    He is the unavoidable problem in higher criticism.

He is the fundamental doctrine of theology.

He is the Cornerstone, the Capstone, and the stumbling Stone
      of all religion.

    He is the miracle of the ages.[6]

The primary reason I've struggled with the love of God is the simple fact that it's like no other love I've ever known. All the other love I've encountered has had something to do with me. My actions somehow preceded the love and proved it conditional. I may have been loved because of my reputation, my possessions, or my talents. But being loved by God is different. His love is unique in that it has *nothing* to do with me. God hasn't chosen to love me because of things about me that he finds lovable. God's love has everything to do with what's true about God. It is God's nature to love, and so God loves me naturally.

GOD'S LIMITLESS LOVE

Those who know me well know I'm prone to exaggeration. No one would call me a blatant liar, but most would agree I have a way of taking the truth and stretching it out a bit. It's refreshing for me to know there is no way possible for me to exaggerate the love of God. It knows no limits or boundaries. The love of God overflows any borders I might try to confine it to.

Those who know me well would also agree that I have always struggled to live in the awareness of God's love for me. (Trust me, they know only part of my struggle!) With my mind I can reason that God's love is true. But in day-to-day life, experiencing that God's immense love for me is the single thing that establishes, governs, and maintains my personal worth is my greatest struggle. I know God's love for me and choice of me is the most significant thing that constitutes my worth, but my default nature is to doubt it. Accepting God's acceptance and letting it become the most important thing in my life have been my greatest challenges. My failures to do so have led to my deadly, never-fast-enough pace.

Today I know there is no need in my life greater than living in the awareness of God's infinite love. If I'm ever going to escape the pattern of maintaining a dangerously busy pace, I must recognize that being the "apple of God's eye" is not merely a nice idea, a worthy goal, or an inspirational thought. It's the one and only name by which God recognizes me and intends to relate to me. This kind of truth must make its way into my heart if I'm to live in any meaningful and lasting degree of freedom.

Almost thirty years ago, while I was still a college student, a little-known nun from India was chosen to receive an award from my school. Stories of her deep spirituality and compassion for others preceded her visit. She was heralded as a future saint among the leaders in her church.

One of the conditions for her coming was that she be given the opportunity to spend a day with a small number of students. Because of my close relationship with the professor whose vision it was to create the award, I was one of the students selected. However, when I considered all the things I needed to accomplish and thought about the waste of time it would be to sit quietly with an elderly nun, I declined the invitation. Because I was so busy and allowed this opportunity to pass, all I can say is that I know some things about Mother

Teresa, but I never knew her. I have been a student of her life, but I missed my opportunity to spend a day with her.

For years I knew many things about God, most of them false. Nothing has revolutionized my life and affected the pace of my living more than the gift of a clearer picture of who God really is. Being given an opportunity to have a clearer look into the heart of Jesus Christ and to begin to understand the wild, passionate, and unconditional love that is in his heart for me is the most life-changing vision my heart has ever held.

Unrestrained, Unexpected Love

Two years ago, while my family was spending a week on the North Carolina coast, I took a walk down a crowded beach. It was one of those walks to nowhere, with nothing particularly on my mind. After walking for quite some time, I noticed a young, darkly tanned boy playing in the shallow surf. I would guess by his size he was about nine years old. With his back turned, he appeared to be having such a great time as he played in the water. As I stood and watched, still twenty or thirty yards away, he suddenly turned, and our eyes met. It was a magical moment. As I looked deeper into his eyes, I could see that he had Down syndrome. At that moment his precious face burst into a smile, and he began to scream what might have been a name, yet I could not understand what he was squealing. Suddenly, with our eyes still locked on each other's, he began running toward me with his arms opened wide. I panicked. But without time to sort out how to best respond, I knelt down and opened my arms as he ran into them. With his arms now wrapped tightly around my neck, he began to kiss me wildly on my lips. After what felt like forever, he loosened his grip, tilted his head back, and with his blue eyes riveted on mine, his face burst again into a smile. I will remember that moment and that smile all the days of my life.

By now there was a lady with a terribly worried expression standing beside us. She tried to apologize, and I tried to explain that all was well.

Moments later I was once again walking alone down the crowded beach. When I returned and began telling my wife about the encounter, I said, "Honey, he kissed me like I've never been kissed before." (I wish I had said, "Honey, how I wish my kisses would feel this way to you and our children," but I didn't.)

For the next several days I couldn't get far from that experience in my mind. Still, I was not certain why or how this incident had so impacted my life. Finally, a few evenings later, sitting alone on our front porch, God spoke to me. "Fil, I'd love to tell you why that experience has such a grip on you. That little boy was a picture of my wild and reckless love for you. The way he looked into your eyes is the way I have always looked at you. That beaming smile on his face is how you make me smile. The way he wildly screamed with glee is how I feel about you. The way he held you in that tight embrace is like mine. The way he kissed you only begins to express the love that is in my heart for you. Fil, you can't imagine how great and infinite is the love that is in my heart for you. I am totally crazy about you. I simply can't take my eyes off you."

Even now as I write about that incredible encounter, my eyes are flooded with tears. I haven't been the same since, nor will I ever again be the same. I've been forever changed by the love of Jesus Christ! It really is one thing to know something in my head and quite another to let it make its way into my heart. Finally, the love of God has begun to settle into my heart.

A. W. Tozer was right. "What comes into our minds when we think about God is the most important thing about us."[7] Nothing else can provide the antidote to an addiction to productivity. Only this clear image of the love of God expressed in the person of Jesus Christ will free us from believing that it's up to us and how well we perform. With God, it's never up to us.

After hearing the story of my encounter on the beach, a close friend posed a haunting question: "Not all of us will have a sandy-haired Down syndrome kid kiss us to death. What are the rest of us to do?"

Pondering his question led to one of my most treasured memories. It was the Saturday evening prior to the last Sunday in Advent. While my family ate dinner, I announced that we would not be going to church the following morning. A huge celebration ended abruptly when I announced that we were going to stay home and have our own family worship. At that moment they began begging to go instead to church.

The next morning we gathered around our Advent wreath and offered our simple worship. After singing a few songs, reading some Scripture, and offering some prayers, we were finished, and everyone made a fast exit, except for my son Lee, who was five at the time.

"Do we gots any dark juice?" he asked. Believing there were some Boppin' Berry Sip-Ups in the refrigerator, he headed for the kitchen, but not before he explained, "I wants to remember Jesus dying."

He returned in a few minutes with the fruit drink under his arm and carrying an end piece from a loaf of bread. He carried the bread in his little hand with great reverence, and with the crust side facing up, he began rubbing the crust and looked at me and offered the explanation, "This is his beard."

Then turning the bread over, he continued to rub it and said, "This is his skin." He tore it in half, and giving me half, we celebrated the broken body of our Lord.

Then he took the Boppin' Berry, drove the straw through the aluminum seal, and explained that they had done this to Jesus. He took a sip and handed it to me so we could share in celebrating the blood of Jesus. And in those holy, Spirit-infused moments, just as he had wished, we remembered the death of Jesus.

No picture more clearly illustrates the love of God than the death of Jesus on the cross. As Brennan Manning has said, the cross of Jesus is the signature of Jesus. It's the ultimate expression of God's love for the world. By dying on the cross, Jesus made it possible for our twisted hearts and minds to be in harmony with his.

I do not understand how, but I believe God intends to accommodate each person's twistedness. God wants to meet us in some exacting way that shows how deep is the love in his heart for us. Perhaps you will find yourself enjoying that harmony with God in the pages that follow.

—POINTS TO PONDER—

1. What words best describe the image that comes to mind when you think about God?

2. What are the primary influences that shaped your view of God? Did those influences help you develop an accurate picture of God or a distorted picture?

3. In what ways has your view of God shaped your life? Have you ever believed that you can control God by your actions—either bringing him joy through doing good things or making him angry through your inactivity or lack of obedience?

4. Have you ever viewed God as an anemic deity who relies on you to get things done?

4

THE LIFE THAT
MAKES US SICK

It All Begins with a Lie

To embrace one's brokenness, whatever it looks like,
whatever has caused it, carries within it the possibility
that one might come to embrace one's healing.

—ROBERT BENSON, *Living Prayer*

I've often heard that a person is as sick as the secrets he or she keeps. I believe this explains why my life has so often made me sick. Secrets harbored deep inside left me feeling isolated, lonely, and afraid. Did I realize harboring secrets was hazardous to my health? Not until years later. And so I did the most effective thing I knew to do to avoid those awful feelings: I stayed constantly busy so I didn't have time to acknowledge feeling isolated, lonely, or afraid. Sound familiar?

FEAR OF THE TRUTH

One day when I was young, my mom left my brother, Steve, and me home alone while she ran some errands. Seizing our newfound independence, my brother and I began to fool around in a manner that would never have been allowed if our mom had been home. Jumping on furniture, throwing pillows, and running from room to room, we were having a blast until I knocked a lamp off the table, shattering the lamp and our fun into a thousand pieces.

When Mom returned, I was frantically cleaning the house. Having already vacuumed, made my bed, and washed some dishes, I was trying to figure out how to wash a load of dirty clothes. Hardly stopping to greet her, I continued with my busyness. "Is there something wrong?" she asked. "This is rather strange...you cleaning the house. Is there something you need to explain?"

Have you ever found yourself driven by guilt, hoping your performance will gain God's acceptance? Have you ever felt compelled to do good to try to make up for your badness in God's sight?

Although I never asked, I suspect my mom discovered the missing lamp long before I was able to muster a confession. After all, a prominent fixture was missing from the house (my brother and I had immediately gathered the broken pieces and thrown them away). I don't remember how long I waited before offering my declaration of guilt. What I do remember is how relieved I felt after telling the truth.

One of my strongest desires has been to tell the whole truth about myself—always. However, one of my biggest fears has been that if I did tell the truth, family and friends would stop loving me. (I do not wish to blame my parents, friends, church, or teachers for the ways in which they imparted this message. However, if I'm honest, I must acknowledge this is where I learned it.) As a result of my fear, there is no one who has been allowed to completely hear what I really think, feel, or believe at my core. And I'm sure I've even tried to keep the truth from myself, but I was usually so good at it, I rarely knew when it was happening.

Fear and Secrets

For the past fifteen years I've been meeting once a week with three other men. We've made some wrong turns, but we do try to keep one another honest. I trust these men as much as any persons I've ever known. I've been brutally honest with them about my fears, hurts, disappointments, frustrations, dreams, and failures. Sometimes, but not all the time. I still have secrets. There are things about me that I'm afraid for them to know. Yet, in those too-few moments when I've dared to risk their rejection or disgust, telling the truth has brought me tremendous relief, even exhilaration. Rather than creating distance between us, my disclosures have drawn us closer.

Why then do I insist on keeping secrets? The answer is that my fears of being known often are bigger than my desires to be known. Along with the fear of rejection, there's this little problem of pride. After all, I want other people to think I have my life together. Yet in the least-edited moments when I'm being honest with myself, I know they know better.

In the previous chapter I described my former, false images of God and the damaging, life-shaping power they wielded. Imagining God as harsh and demanding, I became harsh and demanding, mostly toward myself. Imagining God as angry and disappointed, I got angry and disappointed with myself. After all, if God felt that way toward me, who was I to feel differently?

A dear and trusted friend has often said that when his life on earth has ended and he stands before God, God will ask him just one question: "Did you believe that I always loved you?" God's love determines my friend's beliefs about God's character and the things God values: "Did you believe that I always loved you?"

Where in the world did he get that idea? I wondered. I've always imagined and dreaded that I'd have to account for my every offense, including the day from my boyhood when I uttered the out-of-bounds word while playing basketball with my friends. I still feel the shame of that moment, when I gathered enough self-condemnation to make me want to run off the court and never show my face again. I was sure that this curse word was just the first of many failure-filled,

God-disappointing moments I would have to account for when I stand before the judgment seat of God.

However, as I've wondered many times about the radical proposition of God's love, I've concluded that my friend just might be right. My response to that one question is the only thing I know that will provide evidence about the kind of person I was in this life. If I've lived in awareness of God's radical, unbridled, never-been-kissed-like-this-before love for me, how could I live anything but a loving life in response? The fact that I'm not living that life suggests that I'm still sadly mistaken about God's view of me.

THE DEMONIAC AND ME

A story in the fifth chapter of the gospel of Mark helps me face my driven, broken story. You might recall Mark's account of the chain-shackled, demon-possessed denizen of the graveyard.[1] I used to listen to this story, thinking that I couldn't possibly have anything in common with this naked lunatic. But as I've reflected on my life, I've discovered a few uncomfortable, striking similarities between his life and mine.

The boat Jesus and his friends had been traveling in pulls up to the shore. Jesus leaps off the bow and hits the sand. The disciples bail out of the boat, splashing one another as they tie up, making sure the boat is secure. Jesus looks up, sees a cliff, and says to his friends, "This'll do." Out of nowhere, it seems, steps a demon-possessed man, shouting and gesturing, as if this beach were his private property. As the madman stamps through the sand, headed straight for Jesus, the disciples motion to one another to stand back a safe distance. Jesus inhales deeply and waits until the man and he are face to face. Jesus knows what the lunatic is thinking: *Living with a mental illness is bad enough without all these people seeing that my home is among the headstones.*

I'm pretty sure I know what had the demoniac so agitated. I recall the kind of dread a kid feels on the first day of school as every teacher from first to sixth grade asks every child, "Where do you live?" I'd look down at my feet and mumble, "At 542 Bonham Avenue." Ours was not a prestigious neighborhood or even a desirable one. It was all we could afford, which lowered my status in the view of my classmates. But it was safe and clean, if small. Did I mention there was no status associated with living there?

From my earliest years, knowing that my house and neighborhood didn't measure up, I realized something else would have to become the source of my identity. Otherwise I'd never feel good about myself. The financial resources and natural abilities that others had at their disposal simply were not available to me. I couldn't count on my clothes, grades, athletic ability, or even my physical appearance to win any prizes. Just as the disciples' feet sank in the wet sand that day, I could feel myself sinking beneath the weight of my desire to be recognized as somebody significant.

Middle-school dances were particularly good places to feel dreadfully embarrassed. The problem begins with how you're dressed for the event. The shoes I wanted were the shoes all my friends wanted, the shoes every kid growing up in the Southeast wanted—Bass Weejuns. My parents made it clear there was no way they could afford to buy a pair for me. "Honey, these look close enough," insisted my mom, knowing how angry my dad would be if she bought the real thing. I had to settle for a pair of imitations. I adapted, just as kids everywhere adapt, and discovered, much to my relief, that these were better than my old, worn-out Chuck Taylors. That is, as long as I didn't have to take the shoes off in public.

However, when I arrived at the dance, I discovered, much to my terror, that it was a sock hop! As the name implies, sock hops require that you remove your shoes. Thus I was forced to remove mine, exposing, shamefully, their imitation label. That these shoes were imitations and not the real thing could not have been more obvious than if someone had displayed them on the bandstand under the spotlights. The only thing that could make things worse was the truth that they were mine. Once again, my cover had been blown. "Okay, we'd like to dedicate our next song to the guy with the imitation Bass Weejuns. You know who you are, Fil!"

As an adult, I was still looking for status and an identity, and I thought I had found both in my work. Although my desire to help adolescents know the truth about God was genuine, so was my desire for identity, which I believed was contingent upon being recognized as an effective leader. If my efforts generated good results, I had plenty of self-esteem. Before I knew it, my identity was consumed by my work. Life became a big scoreboard where the points that measured my worth, or in my case, its lack, were being posted. Sadly, I had begun to sell my soul to those who could add or take away points from the scoreboard.

Any activity others deemed successful led me to feel worthwhile. When people referred to me as "irreplaceable," my heart swelled with pride—and relief. To feel good about myself I worked harder and longer, constantly fearing that someday, someone would discover that I was not everything I was working so hard to prove I was. I was now the prisoner of my self-made illusions.

Up for Grabs

The gospel writer Mark makes sure we know the demoniac's life was out of control. "No one could restrain him any more…no one had the strength to subdue him" (Mark 5:3-4).

I know exactly what is being said. There was a time when I could not be still. Life's opportunities and demands presented themselves in steady procession, and I simply could not say no. Lucie begged me to slow down. My children—Meredith, Will, and then Lee—joined in the chorus. Even my supervisor insisted I adjust my schedule. "Sure," I replied and then pursued my work with the same level of obsession. I didn't know I was addicted to the powerful drug of recognition. Although recognition's payoffs felt good at the moment, I was never satisfied. No amount of praise was enough.

Since I often resented the demanding pace, I daydreamed about life scenarios that contrasted dramatically with my daily existence. In my daytime fantasies, life was simple and uncomplicated, and somehow I was completely in control of my life. But instead, reality meant there were always too many things going on, too many demands, and too many needs. Always running behind, I couldn't finish everything I believed I must do. Burdened and guilty for being so inadequate, in my efforts to rev up my personal performance I shamed myself for being unable to respond to all the needs that clamored for my attention.

Why do I—or you, for that matter—tend to equate identity and worth with our activity and accomplishments? The Garden of Eden holds the key. The story of my life had actually been played out in the drama that unfolded in the garden.

Neither the story of Adam and Eve nor our own stories can be understood without first understanding that which God chooses to call *sin.* For as long as I can remember, I've lived with a strong sense that something was wrong in my life—the sin of the singularly focused lie: "You will be like God" (Genesis 3:5). Maybe the serpent repeated his lie five times, each time emphasizing a successive word. "*You* will be like God. You *will* be like God. You will *be* like God. You will be *like* God. You will be like *God.*" Wow! No wonder their heads were spinning. Believing that lie is the very thing that led Adam and Eve to sin.

The fundamental nature of sin is to declare independence from God. And what comes more naturally than thinking we have to make it on our own? But to do that, I needed to become strong and adequate.

No more Mr. Pathetic, weak, limping-along guy, always depending on God. I determined to be strong and capable, not to resort to relying on God for strength, wisdom, and encouragement. I could and would make it on my own.

Reading those words now, I shudder. How could I have been so blind? But thinking about it again, I know how easy it is to be blind, willingly blind, every day.

I remember the stage in my daughter's life when, just like her dad, she began declaring her independence. It was a stiflingly hot July afternoon, and the two of us were running errands. We stopped at the mall, leaving the car windows rolled up while we went inside. Upon our return, I knew the inside of the car would be like an oven. As I opened the door and began to place Meredith in the car seat, she arched her back and insisted that she buckle herself in. Her car seat had been exposed to direct sunlight, and if I didn't assist her the backs of her little legs would be burned by the hot plastic. So I instinctively placed one hand between the car seat and the backs of her legs, holding on to her with my other arm. She thought I was trying to buckle her in, so she fought even more fiercely, forcing my hands away. "I do it, Daddy!" she wailed. She was determined to reject my help, and neither the blistering hot surface of the seat nor my efforts to protect her were going to change her mind.

This remains a perfect picture of my attitude toward God and the foolishness of my choices. I insisted on living life on my terms...even if it meant I'd get burned. I saw myself as self-sufficient, believing I was smart enough and talented enough to handle life on my own. I didn't want to be told what was best for me, even if it meant I'd suffer the consequences.

There in the garden, Adam and Eve believed the lie that they could achieve the same stature as God—and look at the consequences! How could I, one who knew God and the things of God, have fallen prey to the same horrible deception? And I bought the lie so willingly. I was optimistic, at times, in my ability to get better at recognizing self-deception. And I spotted the deception just often enough to make me think that I really could separate God's truth about me from the self-deluding lie. But most of the time I excelled in recognizing my failures, reinforcing my need to—and here's the lie—shame myself with ruthless disapproval. This behavior certainly had a close link with the lie that I needed to be self-reliant, taking over God's rightful role in my life.

"Surely if I try a little harder, I can get my life together. I know I can. I'm just such a loser. In fact, I'm disgusted with myself. Why can't I control my life? Look at me. I'm strong, capable, bright, disciplined. But something's still wrong. I'm so pathetic."

To assure that others would think the best of me, I preferred that they believe a lie about me. For this to happen, I had to convince people I had it all together. In fact, this task became my hardest work. I needed to prove my lovability because no person in his right mind who knew the truth about me could ever love me.

Propping up the lie wore me out. I bought into the deception, and I was paying the consequences. I willingly believed in the Garden of Eden hoax that I, too, would be like God. Believing this leads each person into whatever house of mirrors he or she chooses. Mine was a continual whipsaw: I was cast back and forth between believing that I could solve the problems in my life and believing that there really were no problems to be solved. No matter which lie captured me for the moment, I declared my independence from God, and that, my friend, is sin.

An insightful person asked, "What happened to the break-throughs you experienced years earlier during your hospital stay? Had you simply forgotten what had brought you to that initial state of emotional exhaustion? Had you forgotten the freeing insights you gained?" I wish I had a better answer than yes. Why are life's most important lessons the hardest to hold on to? And why do we sometimes have to learn the hardest lessons more than once?

A Severe Judge

There was one thing I had trouble understanding when it came to the demon-possessed, tomb-dwelling man, and that was his bizarre behavior toward himself. "Night and day…he was always howling and bruising himself with stones" (Mark 5:5). The truth hurts, I've been told, only when it needs to. I guess I needed the pain of this realization: I was just as self-destructive as the madman living in the graveyard. After all, most of what made my life painful and difficult was not any pain or difficulty imposed by others; it was self-imposed.

Think of the harshest, most judgmental person you know. That person doesn't even come close to the severity of my self-judgment. The path to self-hatred was hardened and well worn, like a shortcut across the lawn between two buildings on a college campus. I'm adept at howling and bruising myself. Just ask my wife, Lucie. You don't want to see the despising look I often encountered in the mirror. Whether you're a respectable ministry leader or a tormented graveyard dweller, you don't want your life to feel like an emotional garbage heap. To keep those haunting feelings at arm's length, I got dangerously busy.

For the most part, I was busy doing "good" things. I was meeting with people, leading a ministry, doing my level best to meet real needs. But whenever the dark clouds of self-hatred swirled about me, those around me learned to keep their distance. My wife and children began to fear me, never knowing whether they were going to encounter the sunny, together "public" me or the dark, haunted "private" me.

Deception embodies many paradoxes. One such paradox was that while I was so harsh with the ones closest to me, I could be incredibly tender-hearted toward others. This capacity to be one way in one moment and quite the opposite the next led me to fear that I was schizophrenic. But I wasn't. I was simply giving others what I so badly wanted for myself: a little kindness and tenderness.

A Case of Mistaken Identity

Having watched Jesus and his friends row to shore, get out, and tie up, the demon-possessed man ran wildly toward Jesus, shouting at the top of his lungs, "What have you to do with me, Jesus, Son of the Most High God? I adjure you by God, do not torment me" (Mark 5:7). In other words, "Jesus, my life's a total disaster and now you're going to make it worse. Just get out of here and leave me alone!" How ironic, how sad, for one in such bad shape as the madman to believe that the only One who could make sense of his non-sense life would dare to make it worse. Yet I understand this madness. Blind in my own deception, I was nothing more than a spruced-up version of the tomb dweller. I had a great fear that Jesus might rob me of things I had worked hard to attain. What if he tampered with my friends' approval, stole some of the things I did for fun, or took away some of my pleasure?

For all the years I worked with adolescents and their families I never heard one person say, "My life was going really well until I got involved with Jesus. Then everything just fell apart!" I did, however, hear countless folks tell about the remarkable transformations that occurred when they encountered the unconditional, unbridled, radical love of God.

The love of Jesus Christ is the most powerful and amazing force in life. His love has proven stronger than every rejection, disappointment, or failure I've encountered. His love has proven more durable than every tragedy, worry, or hurt I've endured—more powerful even than my expert self-condemnation.

What's in a Name?

I don't know if the demon-possessed man really wanted to hear what business Jesus, the Son of the Most High God, had with him. But whatever he thought, he wasn't ready for what came next. Jesus asked him, "What is your name?" (Mark 5:9). Anyone else would have presented a defense or rebuttal, but not Jesus. Instead, he simply asked a question. And his question sent the man a message: You matter very much to me, and I want us to be together.

The man replied, "My name is Legion; for we are many" (Mark 5:9). I know the father of a high school girl who jokingly threatened to rename his daughter "Legion," because every time she came from her room she seemed to be a different person. I can relate, not with regard to my children, but to me. For most of my life I've yearned to know who I really am and to be that person all the time. Somehow, I think God has had the same yearning for me.

I am drawn to children who are simply themselves, whether in the company of grownups or other children. They seem to exemplify the wise, old preacher who said, "Be who you *is,* 'cause if you ain't who you *is,* you *is* who you *ain't.*" Sooner than later, it seems, a parent or other adult or maybe a peer or the media get to children with the message that they need to be somebody else. A child stubs her toe, and her mom tells her to stop crying: "Do you want others to think you're a baby? Act like a big girl!" For many this is how the charade parade begins.

A major cause of the frustration and confusion that characterized my life was that I looked in the wrong places for the answer to who I am. I looked to high school students involved in my ministry and wore myself out being the best friend they had ever encountered in order to hear them praise me as a good friend. I looked to the staff and volunteers I worked alongside and did all I knew to do to gain their respect and approval. I looked to my wife and kids to tell me I was the best husband and dad a person could ever hope for. I looked to my extended family and closest friends to tell me I was a godly man, so I did whatever I felt was necessary to gain their approval.

Yet identity, my identity, is something that only *God* can give me.

Only the Inventor can give to the invented its identity, significance, and ultimate purpose. And yet I ran from my Inventor, and everything about my life said, "I don't need help with such matters." I chose to ignore my Inventor's purpose, meaning, and name for me. Somewhere, somehow I started choosing how to figure those things out for myself.

Turning away from my Creator and turning instead to other creatures for my identity was the next logical step. Looking back, I can see how I was programmed from an early age to know more about where I was and what I should be doing rather than who I was and how I was meant to be.

A Child Playing for the Crowd

The questions asked of me when I was young trained me in the things others found most important. "What do you want *to do* when you grow up?" And even if "What do you want *to be?*" was ever asked, my answers invariably fell neatly into career categories—professional athlete, astronaut, fisherman, or fireman—not character categories—a faithful Christian, a philanthropist, a compassionate person, or even a creative person. Having been trained to connect my identity with what I did more than who I was, my identity was to be found in my performance. This resulted in my identity's being reduced to my performance *plus* other people's ratings of my performance. The more audiences I played for, I figured, simply raised my chances for bigger and better ratings, when in fact what was raised were my chances for leading a more confusing life. As Evelyn Underhill put it, I spent most of my time and energy conjugating three verbs: "to want, to have, and to do."[2] I was forever playing to the crowd.

I recall reading many years ago an interview of a member of the Boston Philharmonic Symphony Orchestra. In it the interviewer asked how it feels to get a standing ovation after a performance or a negative

review the morning after. I was initially puzzled by the classical musician's response as she explained how she used to be greatly affected by
the crowd's reception, however, over time had learned to look only for
the approval of her conductor. Her logic was simple; her conductor
was the only person in the crowd who really knew how she was supposed to perform.

A Broken Life Restored

The story of the demon-possessed man concludes with Jesus dealing
most spectacularly with the tragedy this man's life had become. The
solution was unconventional, unpredictable, and unquestionable.
Because God made the demon-possessed man, only Jesus could know
exactly how to solve the mystery of his broken life. After Jesus cast out
the demons, the disciples shoved the boat back off the sand. It was
clear that Jesus was about to leave, and "the man who had been possessed by demons begged him that he might be with him. But Jesus
refused, and said to him, 'Go home to your friends, and tell them how
much the Lord has done for you, and what mercy he has shown you'"
(Mark 5:18-19).

What a radical transformation, from begging Jesus to *leave him
alone* to begging Jesus for the chance to *be with him.* In finding Jesus,
the former madman found his own true identity, and in finding his
identity, he found Jesus. Now that he knew himself as a beloved child of
God and friend of Jesus, he was equipped to live his life. Therefore Jesus
told him to return to his home and live the life he was created to live.

As I've reflected on this story, there are things I still don't understand. (You might notice I didn't mention anything about the method
Jesus used to deal with the demons.) However, it's clear that Jesus
loved the man more than anyone had ever loved the man and in ways
he'd never been loved. I believe this man spent the rest of his life trying to comprehend the dimensions of Jesus' love for him. Most fasci-

nating is the fact that Jesus didn't love this man for any of the reasons I expect to be loved. Jesus loved him, not because he was charming, attractive, useful, or talented. In his former state, the man was none of those things. Jesus' love had to do with one thing only: who Jesus is. It was nothing about the man, and everything about Jesus.

When our son Will was three years old, Lucie and I had a month-long assignment at a Christian camp in New York. I was to be the camp speaker. Knowing my days would be filled once we arrived, Lucie and I decided to take a whole week to drive the trip, allowing us to spend some quality time together as a family. I can still recall how pleasant our journey was. Meals taken leisurely, interesting sights experienced along the way, none of the noise and hurry we knew would await us once we arrived at camp.

As expected, when we arrived I hit the deck running. I spent the first three days in staff meetings. When camp began, I remember sitting in a meeting, aware of someone pacing back and forth at the end of a long hallway to my left. At first, I gave no thought to the person's presence. But as the march continued, I turned and discovered that it was Will. When he passed in my full view, he slowed down and looked in my direction. I was now distracted, wondering what was going on. He kept pacing, so the next time he passed I motioned him to come to me. I pray that I will never forget the look of sheer joy, relief, and delight on his face. First walking and then running toward me, he shouted, "Him wants me! Yes! Him wants me!" After enjoying a full week of nonstop attention, my son was wondering whether I still wanted to be with him.

For most of my life I've frantically paced back and forth, wondering, fearing, and dreading how God feels about me. For the past fifteen years, I've been living in the growing awareness that God wants me to admit my brokenness and let my Inventor heal my severely damaged self-image. It's as if Jesus has taken me by the hand and led me to the real me, the person I truly am, the person he made me to be.

Greenhousing My Soul

My father-in-law has a greenhouse where any plant would be honored to grow. Walking down the rows, it's apparent he knows just what his plants need to thrive. Providing what they require delights and satisfies him. Many of the plants living in his greenhouse are not native to his area, yet he lovingly takes the time to create just the right environment, and then the plant takes over and does what it does best. It grows. He has a lot of respect for the way they grow best.

A healthy, thriving relationship with God is not native to my world. You and I are not native to this world. Therefore, for our relationships with God to flourish, we must take seriously the greenhousing of our souls' relationships with God. I must learn to pay attention and yield to the provision God makes for me as he provides the best environment in which I will grow in this foreign land. My soul's relationship with God will thrive only if I allow God to cherish and nourish me.

———

In the remaining chapters we'll explore six resources God makes available to help us cultivate our relationship with him in the greenhouse of everyday life. God wants to grow us up and nurture our souls. Let's invite him to do just that.

—POINTS TO PONDER—

1. Do you agree that keeping secrets can make you sick? Can you think of an instance in which this was evident in your life?

2. What kinds of secrets are you most likely to keep? Can you detect a pattern in the types of things you are reluctant to admit to others and/or to God?

3. How does keeping secrets affect your significant relationships?
4. How well acquainted are you with your "true self"—the person God created you to be?

Part 2

A PATH OF RECOVERY

5

SOLITUDE

Making Space for God in Your Soul

When you are faithful in [silent meditation]…
you will slowly experience yourself in a deeper way.
Because in this useless hour in which
you do nothing "important" or urgent
you have to come to terms with your basic powerlessness,
you have to feel your fundamental inability
to solve your or other people's problems
or to change the world.
When you do not avoid that experience but live through it,
you will find out that your many projects, plans,
and obligations become less urgent, crucial, and important
and lose their power over you.

—ABBOT JOHN EUDES BAMBERGER TO HENRI NOUWEN

One of the biggest lies we believe as we try to draw nearer to the heart of God is that *we* are responsible for the success of this spiritual enterprise. If God is going to touch our soul, then it's up to *us* to make it happen—as if God's activity operates according to our rules and on our schedule.

Because we long for God and because our past efforts to get close to him haven't seemed to work, let's make a new start. The first necessary step is to discard our earlier assumptions. Instead, let's agree that

God is in charge of everything, including the health of our relationship with him. Our role is to make ourselves available so he can draw near to speak to us and to renew our soul on an ongoing basis. We make this possible by stopping, by seeking solitude, and by keeping quiet. I know it sounds way too simple, even lazy, but that's it.

Just give it a try, and you'll find it's one of the hardest things any of us will ever attempt.

THE FEAR OF SILENCE

When I was growing up, the worst punishment my parents could impose was to have me sit in the dreaded time-out chair. Oh, how I hated leaving my friends and my toys to sit all alone. Who in their right mind wants to be alone?

The dread of being alone only intensified as the years passed. While driving recently, I couldn't help but notice a billboard advertising wireless phone service. *Silence is weird* was the message. I think most people would agree that silence is not the most comfortable setting for any of us.

But why should the absence of noise be so threatening? A friend and pastor expressed his concern some time ago when he heard me say that solitude and silence are among the most important commitments in my life. "We were warned in seminary to be wary of solitude and silence," he explained. "Mysticism is something to be avoided."

It seems silence has gotten a bum rap. It's boring (which explains my childhood hatred of the time-out chair), or it means we have no friends (hence the billboard ad for cellular service), or it's just plain scary (as my pastor friend viewed it). I suppose we fear the unfamiliar.

Fear of the unfamiliar took center stage a few years ago when a group of men from a large church in the South invited me to guide their weekend retreat. I assumed the organizers had explained to the men that they would be spending much of the time in silence. But soon after we started, their bewildered expressions made it clear that the silent part of the retreat was a complete surprise.

After I explained the rhythm of the retreat, one man raised his hand. "Do you mean we're not going to talk this weekend?" "Yes, that's the plan," I replied. With a look of confusion bordering on fear, he again expressed his apprehension. "You're telling me we're going to spend the entire weekend, even share our meals together, without talking?" Awkward silence followed, but something about the way he posed his question seemed profound. "Yes," I said, "but please understand our purpose is to pay attention to God, to see and hear God more clearly. The silence is just a means to that end. Intimacy with God is what we desire."

Another pause, and then he raised his voice in disbelief, "This is *bizarre!* Without a doubt the most *bizarre* thing I've ever heard!" And with that, we entered the retreat and the painful silence of our rooms.

During the course of the weekend, I observed my fellow struggler. By Saturday afternoon he appeared to be settling into the solitude and silence. When the silence ended on Sunday afternoon, the group gathered to reflect on their experience. Several of the men spoke. I wondered what God and my friend had been up to. Finally he raised his hand. "As you might recall," he began, "I was a bit apprehensive when I discovered what we were going to be doing, or not doing, here. I don't remember the last time I felt so threatened and afraid. I'm used to being in total control. I didn't like having my props taken from me. The things I usually count on to keep me busy were taken away: no calls to make, no people to talk to, no appointments to keep, no mail to open, no television to distract me, nowhere to go. All that was left was *me*...the one I'm always trying to avoid.

"But to my great surprise, I wasn't alone. God was with me. I've never enjoyed a more profound awareness of God's presence. God's love for me has never felt so near or real. Once I faced my needy condition, God began to restore and heal me."

Then, just as he'd begun the retreat with a profound question, he ended with another. "Where has silence been all my life? I can't believe no one ever told me how clearly I'd be able to see and hear if I just got quiet, paid attention, and listened to my life."

So Why the Bad Rap?

The negative attitude toward solitude and silence in our culture is as stifling as heat and humidity on a summer afternoon. There have been moments in my life when, after expressing my need to be alone, others felt my request was rude, egotistical, or strange. Most people don't understand the need or ever feel the desire to be alone and quiet. For many it simply feels like a waste of time. Driven people, especially, believe the illusion that nothing is happening when they are quiet and still.

Our world has robbed us of the natural rhythms of silence and solitude. Information, much of which comes audibly, has multiplied so rapidly that it's nearly inescapable. In my home there's a television, radio, CD player, telephone, computer, or some other noisemaker in every room. In my office, where I often go to get away from the intrusions at home, a "sound machine" provides the illusion of silence by drowning the outside noise with the sound of ocean waves breaking on the beach.

Some months ago my youngest child, Lee, and I went camping with friends on an uninhabited island off the North Carolina coast. Getting out of the boat, we discovered a church youth group had already set up camp in our favorite spot, and so for the night we became their neighbors. At first I was disappointed not to be alone with my son and our friends, but when the group began singing around the campfire, I was glad for the positive atmosphere. The next morning I was sad to see most of them talking on their cell phones as they sat around the campfire. In contrast, Lee thought that was so cool to have phones on a campout. Now I'm wondering how long it will be before my son asks for his own cell phone.

The bombardment of words and sounds is relentless, each one clamoring for my attention, leaving me scattered, unsettled, and distracted. Some days my life simply seems congested, as if my entire being is stopped up with a bad winter cold. I sense that something is missing, and underneath all the babble I hear myself saying, "Some solitude and silence could probably help."

While writing this chapter, that congested feeling came over me, and I decided to take a walk. Eventually I wandered into the sanctuary of a nearby church. I found my way into one of the pews, lowered the kneeler, and began to indulge in quiet reflection. Just as I was beginning to settle in, the noise from a vacuum cleaner interrupted the silence. At first I was aggravated. After a few moments though, I thought, *I don't need to get frustrated. I can remain centered. After all, someone's just doing his job.* A few moments later there was another loud noise, one like the scratchy voice of a tinny speaker at a fast-food drive-through lane. The janitor, vacuum still running, was now talking to someone on his two-way radio, the kind that beeps after each person has finished saying what he or she wants to say. Finally I left the sanctuary more convinced than ever that, in our world, opportunities for meaningful silence and solitude are few and far between.

In *The Screwtape Letters,* C. S. Lewis offers an antidote for this congestion as he describes a provocative scene where the ranking demon is reprimanding a junior devil. During the confrontation the junior devil is reminded of two things he permitted the person in his care to do, which led to a terrible outcome—the person's return to the intimacy of his relationship with God. Foolishly, the junior devil allowed the "patient" to take a walk alone *and* read a book for his own pleasure.[1] Lewis's insight into the power of these simple yet transforming acts is remarkable. Before reading on, perhaps it would be a good idea to simply put this book facedown and ask yourself, when was the last time *I* took a walk alone or read a book for my own pleasure?

Walking alone and reading for pleasure are the kinds of vital, life-giving activities that can take place when there is solitude. Yet I've spent most of my days willingly (and even unwillingly) tangled up in life's web of demands, feeling I have no time to spend on such simple pleasures as taking a walk. And even if I thought there was time, why would *I* deserve to drift for just a few moments when so many others have so much to do? What I must continue to try to get into my head is that solitude and silence are not luxuries, but some of life's most vital necessities.

The following adaptation of the Prayer for Quiet Confidence from *The Book of Common Prayer* is just the kind of prayer that I need to carry with me and offer regularly:

> You have taught us
> that in returning and rest we shall be saved,
> in quietness and confidence we shall be strengthened.
> By Your Spirit lift us to Your Presence
> where we may be still and know that You are God.[2]

This past spring I was asking a high-school-aged friend about her summer plans. With enthusiasm she explained her arrangement to care for a deaf neighbor. "What do you do together?" I asked. "One of her favorite things is going to movies," my friend explained. I was a bit surprised. "How could a deaf person enjoy movies?" I wondered out loud. Offering an understanding smile, the girl replied, "She says that without the words and music, she's able to pay closer attention to things I would never notice."

Since then I've wondered, *What am I overlooking as a result of the noise and hurry in my life?* A dear couple spent their thirtieth anniversary on Bald Head Island, a quiet place off the North Carolina coast

with no cars, just bicycles and electric golf carts. On the balcony of
their second-floor room, they sat silently and wrote down every sound
they heard for thirty minutes. They listed thirty different sounds from
as far as half a mile away and as close as the sound of pencils writing
on paper.

THE CONSPIRACY AGAINST SILENCE

A while back I was invited to speak at a Quaker worship service. The
worship began with twenty minutes of uninterrupted singing, at the
end of which everyone took their seats and became very still. Not me.
I fumbled nervously through my bulletin, fearing I might've missed
my cue to stand and speak. Then it dawned on me; they were using
this time as an opportunity to settle down. On the surface, it appeared
that nothing was happening. Yet I wonder if the most significant
moments for some worshipers that day came during the moments of
solitude and silence.

A friend attends a weekly, early-morning service where several
worshipers meet to pray together. Fifteen minutes of silence follows
the morning's hymn and the singing of the psalms and the reading of
God's Word, followed by corporate and individual prayer. My friend
arrived late, after the hymn, the psalms, and the Scripture reading, but
he was on time for the silence. He says those moments are among his
most memorable moments with God.

One of my most grave concerns is that the church has joined
forces with the world in a conspiracy of noise, busyness, and hurry.
The outcome is that we are distracted from a life of intimacy with God
and each other. Most churches are frighteningly busy places, offering
little if any encouragement to adhere to God's counsel: "Be still, and
know that I am God!" (Psalm 46:10). Even in most of the worship
services I attend, little if any space is provided for the silent inward
journey to unfold. Most space that would be available is filled with

spiritual infomercials and announcements to get busy doing something for God. If, as a wise saint once said, religion is what one does with his or her solitariness, then most churches leave little room for religion.

I don't wish to assign sole blame to the church. I admit that I've often been more than willing to accommodate the demand to *do something*. After all, my busyness has helped me perpetuate the message to others and myself that I matter. The busyness, noise, and hurried activity have also given me a sort of shelter to hide in. But sadly, in the process I became addicted to these things and made a conscious choice to live in that deadly, deceitful web.

DYING FOR FRESH AIR

When I was in college, I spent several weeks traveling throughout Japan. I vividly recall the polluted, cloudlike darkness that seemed to hang over the larger cities and the constant struggle involved in breathing the smog-filled air. Glass-sided booths lined Tokyo's streets, available to pedestrians should they want to pop in for a few breaths of fresh air. I remember coming out of one, hoping I'd make it to the next booth without choking on the bitter air. However, as my pace quickened, some pedestrians appeared so accustomed to the smell that they made their way without ever stopping for a breath of fresh air.

The memory of my ducking into those human-size fishbowls to escape the toxic world and for a breath of fresh air is a metaphor for the kind of world I live in and how I can choose to live. Without recognizing what's happening, the toxic environment I live in will kill my soul as surely as the toxic air in Japan would have eventually killed my body. I must be attentive to the rhythm of my life and its need for the fresh air of solitude and silence to survive.

Author Robert Benson realized he was ill-equipped for life in this era, so he devised a theory of life that he calls the "Rule of 21."

Twenty-one minutes is the amount of time that one can go without being interrupted by a telephone call, a knock at the door, or an attack from cyberspace....

Twenty-one days seems to be the maximum number of days that one's life can go smoothly. The average is four, but the limit is twenty-one I think. It's hard to live for more than twenty-one days without a car breaking down, a trip being cancelled, a family member getting sick, a pet dying, a tire going flat, a deadline being missed, or some other thing that scatters all of one's otherwise neatly arranged ducks.

Twenty-one weeks is the absolute maximum amount of time I can go without some meaningful silence and solitude, or else my nerves get shaky, my work suffers, and my relationships start running on empty. That period of roughly one hundred and fifty days is about fifty percent farther than I should attempt to travel without a retreat.[3]

I couldn't agree more! My desperate need, from time to time, is "to go into Arabia." The renowned Presbyterian pastor Bruce Thielman first introduced me to this phrase in a sermon he preached almost thirty years ago. Over the years I've occasionally been drawn back to his sage wisdom, and I remain indebted to him for his insights. The expression is found in a letter Paul wrote to the early church in Galatia. In describing his radical, life-altering encounter with Jesus Christ while en route to Damascus, Paul explained:

You have heard, no doubt, of my earlier life in Judaism...violently persecuting the church of God...trying to destroy it.... But when God, who had set me apart before I was born and called me through his grace, was pleased to reveal his Son to me...I did not confer with any human being...but I went away at once into Arabia. (Galatians 1:13,15-17)

Paul points out that after this life-altering encounter, he took some time to get away and sort through the issues in his life, to find what mattered most. He "went away at once into Arabia" so he could think about the ultimate questions of who God was, who he was, and what their relationship meant. I suspect Paul's retreat to Arabia was as clarifying for Paul as Jesus' forty days in the desert.

WHOLEHEARTED LISTENING

As I ponder the season of solitude and silence in Paul's life, I imagine him sitting alone in the desert, listening for a sound that's far more subtle than the whining of the desert wind, quietly and wholeheartedly listening for the whispering voice of God. When I reflect on those occasions when I've sensed that God was speaking to me, I've always found God's voice to be a quiet, nondemanding voice. God doesn't *insist* that I listen. God never speaks with raised voice. A friend of mine, a missionary to Africa, translates the reference to God speaking to Elijah in 1 Kings 19 as "a thin silence." God's voice wasn't heard in the noise of the powerful earthquake, the wind, or the fire; God's voice was heard in *the thin silence.*

With my mind's eye I can see Paul sitting in Arabia some nights until very late, accompanied only by the desert stars. And there, not writing, not planning, not traveling about, not preaching...not doing *any* of the things he's most known for today...he quietly carved out the deep convictions of his soul. In solitude he hammered out the beliefs on which he would build the rest of his life. He wrestled with the things of God until God possessed him and he possessed God. Later, in referring to that experience, he summed it up with the single phrase: "I went away at once into Arabia." After he'd been with God, what more could he have said?

"Going into Arabia" and communing with God is the single most important, most difficult thing I've ever chosen to do. Yet I know of no other antidote for the plague that threatens all of us. The "barren-ness of busyness," more than anything else, has robbed my days of meaning and a sense of God's presence. An endless round of appoint-ments and responsibilities and assignments and details wears me down. I'm not opposed to hard work. But I am opposed to running long and hard in a good-for-nothing race.

I am learning to recognize that when there's no time for soli-tude and silence, my activity ceases to be effective. Without listen-ing for that voice in the thin silence, my ministry activity lacks power. Without silence, my words lose meaning. When solitude and silence are absent from my life, the best of my intentions warp badly.

The one quality the great saints all share is their attentiveness to God in solitude. These are women and men whose hearts were seized by the power of a great affection. They are people for whom nothing is more important than to wait for God to speak softly into their lives. As I write these words, the longing to be the kind of person these saints were is rekindled, and I'm compelled to ask God to protect that "quiet stream" in my heart, where the things that happen are the things that matter most.

Going into Arabia is about being alone, quiet, and entering into the place of prayer. Going into Arabia is about listening to my soul and listening to the conversation between my soul and God. It's when the deepest part of me reaches out for the deepest part of God. Taking solitude and silence seriously is one of the surest ways I know to put some worth on my soul, a worth that, perhaps, is the dimension of my life I ignore most often.

WHAT'S A SOUL WORTH?

While watching the movie *Bedazzled,* I stumbled upon an intrigu-ing insight into our disregard of the soul. The devil, played by the attractive and seductive Elizabeth Hurley, offers one of the main characters, played by Brendan Fraser, seven wishes to use however he sees fit. The only stipulation is that he must give his soul to the devil, to which he responds, "I can't give you my soul!"

"What are you…James Brown?" she asks. "What's the big deal? Have you ever seen your soul? Do you even know what it is?"

"Of course! It's the thing that…umm. It follows you around."

To which the devil cunningly replies, "Can I tell you something? Souls are overrated. They don't ever do anything. Has yours done anything for you lately? It's like your appendix. You won't even miss it."

Pausing for a moment, he then responds, "Hey, if it's so useless, how come you want it so much?"

Then, with a knowing smile, the devil replies: "Aren't you the clever one?"[4]

One of the most puzzling and sad phenomena I've seen is how easily I place so little value on my soul. Yet, Evil places a high price tag on my soul and continues its attempts to entrap it. The angels place such worth on my soul that there's not been a celebration greater for them than when my soul was rescued. And Jesus Christ gave his *life* to salvage my soul. But for most of my life, I haven't gone into Arabia long enough or far enough to know that I have a soul of great value, much less how to protect and care for it.

I'm not alone in devaluing the soul. As we invest time and energy meeting all the demands we encounter, we are harassed by the need to always go faster. In so doing, we become so consumed with the *external* realities of our world that we begin ignoring the *internal* realities of our life. We lose connection with our soul. I speak from hard experience: I became the busy, driven, angry, superficial, and cynical Fil Anderson. I became a collection of the symptoms of a soul that had fallen into serious neglect, much to the delight of Evil.

THE RHYTHMS OF JESUS' LIFE

The life of Jesus Christ, the One I claim to follow, stands in sharp contrast with my life. When I look at the days that made up his life, I can't help but notice his unswerving devotion to solitude and silence coupled with a God-guided tenderness and compassion for the people he met. What made him care so much about individual people? What caused his heart to reach out to the heart of every person he met?

I suspect Jesus' life was regulated by a deep inner silence. His soul was listening to his Father...always. In the deepest recesses of his being, he was silent, never asserting his own agenda. Jesus lived with remarkable detachment. He didn't seek creature comforts or the temporal pleasures of the world, although the things of this world were easily within reach. His ability to live with a remarkable detachment allowed him to overcome the pull of routine, monotony, and weariness, and gave birth to a lighthearted serenity, a space open for every encounter. This was the food and drink "you do not know about," which he mentioned to a group of disciples who were baffled that he wasn't hungry.[5] Jesus was always receptive to the will of his Father.

In the first chapter of Mark's account of the life of Jesus, I'm fascinated by the rhythm reflected in a typical day. Jesus began this day in the synagogue, it being the Sabbath, and afterward was confronted by the needs of those around him. Mark sets the scene: "They brought to him all who were sick or possessed with demons. And the whole city was gathered around the door. And he cured many who were sick with various diseases, and cast out many demons" (Mark 1:32-34). Mark continues by describing how Day Two began, "In the morning, while it was still very dark, he got up and went out to a deserted place, and there he prayed" (verse 35).

There it is! In the middle of sentences filled with activity—healing desperately sick people, casting out evil spirits—Jesus seeks solitude.

How else could a person handle everything a bucket brigade of disciples can throw at him and still travel from town to town on foot, proclaiming his message, unless "while it was still very dark, he got up and went out to a deserted place, and there he prayed."

The rhythm of Jesus' life is the most remarkable thing to those who are fully committed to accomplishing the most important things. This group includes those whom we call saints as well as entrepreneurs and business executives and moms and dads and you and me. Check it out for yourself. Although Jesus was crowded by noise, busyness, and multitudes of got-to-have-it-now people, none of that threatened him. Neither did the noise, the demands, nor the crowds distract him from his constant communion with his Father. In the eye of the daily storm, he knew the inner quiet of peace and focus. In the center stage of engagement, he would withdraw. In the midst of being with others nonstop, he knew quiet and solitude. There's a reliable saneness to the cadence of Jesus' life. Seeking solitude and silence was his standard practice, and so it must be for me and for you.

Just as Jesus escaped to solitude, and just as Paul went to the desert to be trained by God, "Arabia" is that sacred place where our heart is formed. The "little cell" of my heart is where I confront my spirit until it is brought into harmony with God. It's the place where I temper my devotion, make promises to God, and hear with my soul's ear the promises God makes to me. Arabia is where my deepest soul beliefs are forged and sustained. We need regular trips to Arabia.

A New Definition of Discipline

Recently I was listening to a friend describe the relentless pace of his life and all that he feels compelled to do. After a while I asked, "Does the care of your soul's relationship with God feel like just another thing you have to add to your long list of things to do?" "Exactly; that's it," he answered.

"How would it feel to think of your time with God as a day at the beach?" I probed. With a puzzled look, he replied, "I think that would be awesome. But what are you talking about?"

"You begin by sitting down in a quiet place," I explained. "Then you bask in the bright light and warmth of the sun. There's nothing left for you to do but wait. So it is with God." Oftentimes I tell those who have asked me to guide them on a silent retreat that the two most important things for them to do are to show up and shut up. It's that simple.

Sitting silently and waiting. This is the pattern of encountering God that we see as a model from Old Testament times, in the life of Jesus, and in the lives of the church's earliest leaders. However, this is not how most of us have been taught to think of our relationship with God. When I began to follow God, I was told there's no way to be a disciple without discipline. Just as in sports, the arts, academics, or any other endeavor, I learned I must be diligent and work at it. There must be consistent, disciplined activity. Following Jesus was a challenge, a contest, and one I would either win or lose. But enjoy it, like a day at the beach? Never. Sit quietly and let God approach me without my hastening to do everything I could to chase him down? Are you out of your mind!

More recently I'm beginning to understand that, in my life with God, the word *discipline* means the endeavor to create space in my life in which *God* can act. Discipline means being intentional about preventing everything in my life from being filled up. The diligent watchfulness guards my soul from intrusions that crowd out God.

Marking off space for God to be at work is a challenge because God likes doing things with me that I hadn't counted on. He likes to decide the agenda rather than docilely going along with my carefully scripted list of activities. If I leave God too little space, the desires God has for me and for our time together simply don't happen. This is the why of solitude with God. I simply make room for God to do what only God is able to do. Yet the excuses I make (to myself and to others) for not making this space are endless. Why would I want to cheat myself out of God's deepest longing for me? Is it because I don't trust God? Is it because I'm addicted to being in charge? Is it because I'm simply afraid to let go and rest in the silence of God's presence?

If I am ever to enjoy a rhythm of solitude and silence, I will always need to exert some effort. However, the effort is not to be building outwardly but to protect that little cell of my heart, that part of me where God and I get to be together—to protect it and then to find the solitude where God will enter and spend time with me.

Talking with God Alone

When Paul escaped to Arabia, he reported later that he didn't confer with any human being. Instead, he was with God, alone. I regret how often I have chosen to consult with others rather than with God. It just always seemed so much easier to sit down and talk with someone I could see.

In the isolated silence of the Arabian desert, Paul was able to hear truth descend into the recesses of his heart. I imagine Paul discovered that solitude and silence unite more deeply than words, allowing one to move from communication to communion.

It's significant to note that Paul wrote about his desert experience twenty-five years after the most defining event of his life. Twenty-five years of living with God as his constant companion had unfolded since that moment when he was blinded by the bright light of Jesus Christ's love, mercy, and forgiveness. During those intervening years, Paul had confronted monumental challenges: He'd been beaten, shipwrecked, thrown into jail, and yet he had persevered. It's obvious that Paul, like Jesus, must have maintained an ongoing commitment to a rhythm of solitude and silence. Otherwise, I'm convinced the pressures and demands of his life would have depleted him.

When I was a kid, one of my favorite toys was an inflatable punching bag with the likeness of a Disney character on the front. It was tall, with a high center of gravity, but was weighted at the bottom so it would maintain an upright position despite attempts to knock it over. For the same reason that kids everywhere punch or kick a blow-up character, I would punch or kick that bag and marvel at its ability to bounce back for more.

One day when I was unable to resist the urge to know the secret to my punching bag's resiliency, I cut it open with my dad's pocket-knife and found at the base a bag of sand, what we call ballast. Years later I learned the value of the ballast of the soul. When I meet God in solitude and silence, he adds ballast into my life. I have strength to live and face life's challenges with confidence in God's nearness and provisions. I can take a punch and return for more.

A DEADLY THREAT

Years ago I was given a list of instructions, purportedly written for those preparing to travel to the jungle regions in South America. The title was "What to Do If Attacked by an Anaconda." I'm doubtful that these instructions would actually be helpful if one were attacked, but they make an excellent point. The instructions were as follows:

> If an anaconda attacks you, do not run. The snake is faster than you are.
>
> Lie flat on the ground.
>
> Put your arms tight against your sides and your legs tight against one another.
>
> The snake will come and begin to nudge and climb over your body.

Do not panic. [This I admit, would have never entered my mind!]

After the snake has examined you, it will begin to swallow you from the feet end. Always from the feet end.

The snake will now begin to suck your legs into its body. You must lie perfectly still. This will take a long time. [I am not certain whether this is a reference to the snake's sucking of your legs or the lying still part.]

When the snake has reached your knees, slowly and with as little movement as possible reach down, take your knife, and very gently slide it into the side of the snake's mouth, between the edge of its mouth and the snake's head.

As I recall, it was these last two instructions that really got my attention the first time I read this list.

Be sure your knife is sharp.

Be sure you have your knife.[6]

I don't imagine an anaconda will ever attack me, but I've nonetheless spent a good bit of time reflecting on these instructions and their implications for my life. Sometimes I'm aware, and other times I'm clueless, that things in life are ready to swallow me. There are things that are ready to squeeze out of me all the good that God has put there. By God's good grace, I've begun to understand the way to deal with those things is to be still, to be quiet, to have a plan, and to know what I'm going to do and the way I'm going to do it when the threats appear. The place where I learn to lie still and cultivate a plan is during the solitude and silence that await me in my own Arabia.

Overcoming the Threat

Once I began to acknowledge the need for solitude and silence there remained a storehouse of excuses as to why it's not practical. You might recognize some of these from your own attempts to be still and quiet before God:

"I never know where to begin."

"When I get quiet my mind begins to wander."

"I can't stay awake."

"My prayers always lead me to begin thinking about people I need to see or work I need to complete."

"When I begin to get quiet, the noise in my head becomes like a roar."

"My house is too noisy to find a quiet place."

"I can't get up early enough or stay up that late when the kids are in bed."

I won't pretend to speak for you, but in my heart, at the deeper, personal level of what's going on inside, there are other reasons. The biggest reason I have shunned silence and solitude is so that I don't have to face the most critical, demanding, and difficult person in my life: me. Being quiet and alone offers me the opportunity to confront one of the very real paradoxes of my life: the reality that although I am a social animal, I have a profound and vital life that is unto itself, suggested by such words as *individuality, integrity, soul.* As long as I'm surrounded by other people, tasks, and responsibilities, I can avoid an encounter with me. That's why, once I am alone, the greatest challenge is to resist the urge to pick up a book, listen to music, or busy myself with some other preoccupation. Of all the relational challenges I've faced, the most difficult companion by far I've had to learn to live with is me.

I've also avoided solitude and silence because they somehow remind me of my imminent death. While busyness, activity, and hurry are signs that life is very present, being still and alone are signs to me that life on this earth is ended. Motion helps me evade the reality that my physical life will someday come to a complete halt. When I'm in silence and solitude I must confront the question, Is there more to life than just my life? Is there a bigger meaning to it all? Perhaps this is why the father of modern monasticism, Saint Benedict, as Parker J. Palmer has suggested, pointed to the need to "keep your own death before your eyes each day."[7]

Often I've avoided making space in my life for solitude and silence because it feels like such a waste of time. After all, most of my experience with silence has left me feeling like nothing significant occurred. I suspect the greatest reason I've avoided solitude is my fear of change. I'm no fool. I know that there'll be consequences if I take time for solitude and silence. I realize that if I get alone and quiet, the mask that covers the illusion of my significance might be removed. I'm aware that the silence might call to mind my latent misgivings, guilt feelings, and the strange, disquieting anxiety that can companion me. However, I'm learning that if I work through my initial doubts or fears and settle into solitude and silence, the intimacy with God that my heart yearns for is born.

My excuses seem reasonable, and yet they are nothing more than avoidance. If I'm ever going to enjoy the benefit of "going into Arabia," I'll have to face my resistance and exert some effort. The key is to be intentional and start where I am. I will not get there if I don't deliberately reserve time each day for God and God alone.

SIMPLE STEPS TO SOLITUDE

If you're as hungry for God as I am, here are simple actions that you can practice to invite God to speak to your soul:

Practice gratitude, thanksgiving, and momentary prayer. Claim the little solitudes that already exist in your day. Before getting out of bed, I typically take a few moments to greet God with gratitude for waking me up and providing the gift of another day. My morning shower has become a time for asking God to keep my thoughts and actions pure throughout the day. Mealtime prayers have become a meaningful time not only for offering thanks but also inviting God to join the conversation around the table. If I'm eating alone, I invite Jesus to be my companion. Time alone in the car has become a special time of communion with God when I've chosen to turn off the radio and phone, listening instead for the voice of God. Waiting for an appointment or at a traffic light can be an opportunity to "wait upon the Lord" in silence. At the end of the day, gently reflecting on the ways in which God has shown loving care for me has offered great encouragement.

Read encouraging words, or listen to music. Sometimes it softens my soul to read a few encouraging words from the Scriptures or some other devotional writing, such as *A Testament of Devotion, The Practice of the Presence of God, The Sacrament of the Present Moment,* or *Experiencing the Depth of Jesus Christ.* Other times I find that music helps. Neither the words of songs nor the structure of the music is intended for insight or analysis but rather as a means of focusing my attention on the One with whom I sit.

Use your lunch break. Use a lunch or coffee break to intentionally be alone with God. Sometimes I use the time to reflect on one of the many stories in the Scriptures that took place at mealtime.

Find special places for solitude. I'm always on the lookout for a suitable place to be alone. I find that the space I'm in can be a huge help to open up space in my soul for God. Just a few blocks from my home is a city park that has become a great getaway spot. Many churches have adjacent chapels that are usually open and often empty. Within an hour from my home are numerous retreat facilities that are available for daylong, overnight, or extended times of retreat.

Focus your prayer. A constant challenge to intentional prayer is our tendency to be distracted, which wars against focused prayer. The distractions can be external or internal, and both shift our mind and spirit away from God. When I am bombarded with distractions, or when it begins to feel that nothing is happening or I'm wasting my time, it helps to pray for patience and to focus on my desire for intimacy with God. This is a good time for centering prayer, which can be described as letting go of all competing distractions until we are fully present to God. At other times when I feel distracted or frustrated, it settles my soul to gently repeat a certain word or phrase (*Abba, Jesus, love,* or "God, I belong to you"). Also valuable is the Jesus Prayer, a prayer you can pray throughout the day. It is simply: "Jesus Christ, Son of God, have mercy on me."

Stop, sit, wait. Remember that God is responsible for the relationship with you. Your role is to open spaces where he can commune with you. As such, solitude and silence are more about what we "undo" than what we "do." I often recall a story Sue Monk Kidd tells about her experience on a retreat. After a failed attempt at sitting still in silence, she observed a monk enjoying apparent success. When she asked him how he could sit so still and do nothing, he informed her that she had bought into the myth that waiting and doing nothing are the same. "When you're waiting, you're not doing 'nothing,'" the monk told her, but rather, "you're doing the most important something there is."[8]

Seize the opportunities that are available. Sometimes I simply stay up a little later or get up a little earlier to find a few moments of solitude. Being intentional about communion with God sometimes involves a schedule shift or special accommodation to allow things to happen.

Schedule some space into your day. Whenever possible, I schedule my day with some flexibly built in. It can be incredibly freeing to enjoy a few minutes between tasks or appointments. I often use this time to reconnect with God's presence in the midst of a busy day as well as to gather my thoughts for the next meeting or task. I find in those few moments that my awareness of God's presence is much more keen.

Drop all expectations. Time with God isn't an assignment to be graded. Neither is it a means to an end. The goal is not greater peace of mind or a lessening of anxiety or self-improvement. The goal is to meet with God and possibly to hear from God. So drop all preconditions and let go of any expectations. Giving your attention to desired results seems to work against the results you desire.

Slow down. Often the pace of life pulls me away from my awareness of the Lord's nearness. To deal with life's fast pace, I try to walk, drive, and even eat more slowly. I try to pay attention to what is happening inside no matter what is going on around me. When I do this, I become more aware of the little cell of solitude and silence within me.

Exercise the body and the soul. Often I use my times of physical exercise for silence and solitude. Taking a walk or going on a hike and using the time to notice the sights and sounds of God's creation can be an excellent help in maintaining a clear awareness of God's presence.

GOD'S RESPONSIBILITY

While I hope the list of suggestions is helpful, I offer it reluctantly. A to-do list could wrongfully lead us to think that intimacy with God is our responsibility. I have to guard against this becoming one more thing to add to my already overwhelming list of things to accomplish. It's essential that I understand the health of my relationship with God is ultimately God's responsibility. My responsibility is providing space for solitude and silence so that God may attend to the needs of my soul. I'm just the innkeeper making room for the Guest.

A few years ago I detected once again that the quiet had been seeping out of my life. Burdened by how little time I had spent alone, I decided to get up extra early the next morning, guaranteeing no distractions. Upon waking, I dragged myself out of bed, feeling the weight of responsibility for my relationship with God upon my shoulders. Shortly after settling into my little cell, I heard feet on the stairs that signaled one of our children had awakened. Frustrated and in a rage, I asked God, "What's it going to take for me to be with you?" In just a moment the door opened and my younger son, Lee, peeked inside the room. Reading the disappointment on my face, he said, "I don't want to disturb you; I just want to be with you." In a moment of grace, I gave up on my time alone with God and chose instead to be with my son, realizing that the pace of my life had taken its toll on our time together. We curled up on the sofa as I held him close and tenderly rubbed his back. Settling into this delightful time of companionship, I believe I heard God speaking to me. "It's all right, Fil. You give him what he needs and let me give you what you need."

Too often I wrongly view solitude and silence as a time for me to care for God. How foolish can I be? God doesn't need me to take care of our relationship. Instead, I need to create space for solitude and silence in order for God to be able to do the caring and nurturing.

Many times at the beginning of a retreat I've told participants that my son Lee wouldn't have a clue what to make out of the solitude and silence I talk about. And so he'd just *be* there. He'd find the woods or a stream or a tree to climb or a hammock to lounge in, and he'd be happy. Sometimes he'd get bored and wonder what to do. He might complain about the waste of time or no television, but soon he'd again be occupied or content to simply waste the time *being* there. That's how we open space in our soul for God to care for us.

———————

If the teeth are to be extracted from the relentlessly demanding pace of life, I must face the reality that the threats to my moments of solitude and silence are real. Nothing less than an unswerving devotion to regularly returning to my little cell will do. As long as I choose to maintain an active and noisy soul, my view of God will be clouded. But when stillness and solitude get to accomplish their work and usher me into the awareness of the presence of God, then I find that my soul is not only still and recollected but is overwhelmed in an act of reverence and worship by God's own presence.

—POINTS TO PONDER—

1. What is the typical rhythm of your day or week? How do you relax? Do you find it difficult, guilt-producing, or wasteful to relax? Or do you find it to be renewing?
2. What comes to mind when you hear the word *solitude?* Does the prospect of being completely alone make you uncomfortable, or do you welcome the opportunity?
3. If solitude is not part of the rhythm of your life, what do you feel you're attempting to avoid or resist?
4. Referring to solitude, author Frederick Buechner wrote, "The quiet there, the rest, is beyond the reach of the world to disturb. It is how being saved sounds."[9] After pondering these words for a few quiet moments, how do you feel?

PRAYER

Living in the Mystery and Wonder of God's Presence

Prayer is the test of everything;
prayer is also the source of everything;
prayer is the driving force of everything;
prayer is also the director of everything.
If prayer is right, everything is right.
For prayer will not allow anything to go wrong.

—THEOPHAN THE RECLUSE, *The Art of Prayer*

During the fall of a recent election year, I was invited to speak on prayer to a group in Winston-Salem, North Carolina. On the same night a presidential debate was taking place on the campus of nearby Wake Forest University. As I approached my destination, I began to see the extraordinary safety measures being taken to protect the two candidates. Police officers, Secret Service agents, and other law-enforcement personnel were positioned just about everywhere.

Observing this impenetrable shield of protection, I was struck by the contrast between it and my unrestricted access to God. This Holy Other, this Lover of my soul, invites me to approach him, often urging me to linger, to remain with him. With God practically begging me to stop by and share some unguarded conversation, why do I continue to resist the plunge into unspeakable intimacy with him?

Prayer is the privilege of every human to touch God. It's the ever-available opportunity to pour out what's on our hearts before the King of the universe, the Creator of all things, the All-Knowing Sovereign. Why then does practically everyone, committed Christians included, struggle so much with prayer?

I won't attempt to speak for you, but I know what's in my heart. The easy rationalization is that I resist this open invitation because I'm usually in a horrible hurry. Yet God never raises his voice…and God never, ever hurries. I sure do. I want quick results no matter what I'm doing. Who in their right mind doesn't?

But when I have the guts to come clean, to be entirely honest, what I really want, more than anything, is to be in control. I want God to move at the pace I set. I much prefer prayer to be like driving through the pickup lane at a fast-food restaurant. I want to place my order, drive around to the window, and pick up whatever I'm in the mood for at that moment. I want to be handed, in a convenient package, exactly what I ordered. (*Ordered* is an intriguing word to use when speaking with God, don't you think?) Sometimes I even wish prayer had an express lane, fifteen items or fewer, and no checks please. If there are two things I have trouble with, they are having to wait and not getting what I order.

At least that was me fifteen years ago. If I could have looked into the heart of God back then, I'm certain I would have found an open wound—God aching over my detachment, indifference, and pre-occupation. I was big into my agenda and disconnected from God's longing to spend time with me. I suspect God wept over my refusals to accept the lavish and incomparable gift of prayer. He must have been baffled by my attraction to things that offered appallingly less, even things that were opposite to what his deep affection affords. Like a jilted lover, God longed for my fidelity.

Still, I invested my life in the pursuit of temporal rewards—the accolades of others. As I neglected God, I struggled with great shame and embarrassment. In fact, my failure with prayer, more than any other aspect of my friendship with God, was a constant reminder that my spiritual life was far from what God desired. I was an absolute bundle of paradoxes. I yearned for prayer to be more central in my life, and yet I ran from it. I lamented that I should pray more, and then filled my days with frantic activity.

God's gift of prayer was an incredible opportunity, and I squandered it. Like the prodigal son, I fled the home where I had everything I needed, this home that prayer would have afforded me. Incredibly, I moved to a far country—a country of noise and crowds, of push and pull, of disappointment and constant pressure, of the dread of coming up short, of revealing myself a failure. As did the prodigal, I desperately needed to come to my senses and return home to the ceaseless intimacy I had been so generously offered with no strings attached. I needed to believe in my deepest parts that my Father was waiting longingly and patiently, yearning to receive me with open arms.

GOD'S PATIENT EMBRACE

During the closing session of a retreat, the group was seated in a circle. As they began telling stories of their solitude encounters with God, I observed an expectant mother adoringly rubbing her tummy. Her face was radiant. Almost embarrassed, I looked away toward the others in the circle, but when my eyes returned, I saw her reaching underneath her shirt to make closer contact with the little one growing inside, the one she was longing to embrace.

This tender image has become a metaphor for the longing within God's heart, the longing for me to settle down, to give in to God's tender and loving care, to stop wriggling out of God's embrace. I am foolish to resist, yet shy about yielding. The benefits of being safe with God are incomprehensible. We were made for this intimacy. Hence the utter lunacy of resisting the God who patiently waits.

Over the past several years, by an act of God's mercy and grace, I've begun to understand the key that unlocks the door to God's heart: My intended place with God is constant prayer. If I'm ever going to enjoy the life God offers me (and if I hope to ever recover from my addiction to work and busyness), I must comprehend the necessity for prayer and devote myself to a life of ceaseless praying.

A LIFE FRAMED BY PRAYER

The life of ceaseless prayer became direct experience in my life the first time I visited Mepkin Abbey, a Trappist monastery hidden along the placid Cooper River of South Carolina. I approached the secluded grounds by way of a half-mile entranceway lined with ancient live oaks laced with gray Spanish moss. White Cherokee roses and an array of azaleas bordered the forest, which was lush with pine, yucca, jasmine, and palmetto. The beauty left me almost speechless.

The monastic community there is linked to the centuries-old Christian tradition of the solitary life of prayer. The rhythm and order of life was thoughtfully designed centuries ago for living in deep and intimate communion with the mysterious presence of the living God. Seven times daily the monks of Mepkin Abbey gather to sing the psalms, focus their lives on the Word of God, celebrate the Eucharist, and offer prayers for the world, each other, and for you and me.

They invited me to join them in the rhythm of their day and to go with them into their sacred space, to offer prayers, theirs and mine. At first I was mostly aware of the things that were different about their lives. Their dress was simple, as was their diet. They were celibate. They very rarely spoke, having taken vows of silence. They went to bed at an incredibly early hour and rose at a time I'd call "ungodly." Although I couldn't visit their living quarters, I was sure there were no televisions or cell phones. None had a pager or even a portable radio. They never hurried anything. How different my life was from theirs.

Nonetheless, they never did anything that made me feel my life was inferior to theirs.

After several days of living among them, I became more conscious of how much more our lives could be alike. Just like you and me, they have a vocation. And like us, they have chores. Like other Christians, they live in a community with others, some whose company they appear to enjoy and others they seem to struggle to tolerate. Sadly, the most striking difference between their lives and mine was how seriously they had taken God's summons to never stop praying.

On my way home I had to confront a familiar question: What holds me back? Why could I not live a life framed with ceaseless prayer? I could no longer use the circumstances of my life as an excuse. Certainly the lives of these monks were very different from mine. But the difference had less to do with superficial things like wardrobe, food, and surroundings and *everything* to do with what happens when it's time to pray. When their appointed times for prayer occur, the monks drop whatever important thing they're involved in. Prayer immediately becomes the most important thing. And the rest of the time, when they are going about their other obligations, chores, and joys, they remain centered in prayer as they maintain an ongoing awareness of God's presence. That was the linchpin difference between their lives and mine. Even on those rare occasions when I had begun my day having thoughtfully determined when I would stop and pray and how I would remain aware of God's presence the rest of the time, most days I allowed other things to take precedence over prayer.

To put an end to these struggles, I had to honestly answer a few simple questions: What do I long for so deeply that I can taste it? What do I feel I can't live without? The truth became apparent. My life was driven by my desire to have all that I desired. And there were always too many choices, obligations, and distractions—so my life was distracted and fragmented.

In my heart I truly wanted to be a person who prayed, yet I also wanted to listen to the seductive voices that spoke to my craving for prestige, gratification, power, and influence. Seeking fulfillment in the wrong places had left me running on empty. I knew if I was to ever become a faithful companion to Jesus, remaining with him in prayer, I must reject the lesser voices. I must give full attention to his voice, which calls me to the narrow road, to the life of ceaseless prayer.

Over the years, every time I would encounter John Staggers, a very dear friend, he would grab me by the shoulders, look deep into my eyes, and ask the same question: "Mate, is Jesus enough for you today?" Sadly, I was never able to truthfully answer yes. The monks at Mepkin Abbey have the answer. They have decided to want only one thing: God. And on those days when God is not their one and only desire, they at least want to want God.

MOVING BEYOND FAKE PRAYER

I know that I'm to live a life of continuous prayer but not the life of a monk. (This revelation brought great sighs of relief from my wife and children.) An accurate translation of the biblical words "pray always" is "come to rest." This rest has little to do with an escape from difficulty, conflict, pain, or too much stuff to do. Rather, it's a way of resting in God amid my sometimes dull and dreary, and at other times intense, daily struggles. I will never be free of life's routines and difficulties. Nonetheless, this "coming to rest" emanates from unceasing prayer and must become the guiding focus of my life.

Prayer as a guiding focus of life is far different from rules and disciplines. In the past, my efforts to calm my unrest and banish my addiction to work fell far short of moving me any closer to a life of prayer. The dictatorship of my schedule, by itself, was enough to keep me from stopping to pray. How could I spend significant time in prayer and still hope to accomplish all that I wanted to? Again, my desire for accomplishment outweighed my passion for God.

Another big part of the problem was my twisted image of prayer. I had spent most of my life thinking of prayer as an intellectual exercise, a practice of speaking to or thinking about God rather than just being with God. This is the traditional evangelical view—approaching prayer as a rationalistic exercise. It led to untold sessions of empty and meaningless monologue. I would say my prayers and then hurry to the next item on my agenda, never giving God a chance to reply. Back then, prayer was a soapbox that afforded me an opportunity to get some things off my chest with God as my captive audience. But I completely missed the rich opportunity to listen for God's voice, which was far more important than my self-serving laundry lists of requests and complaints. I shamelessly disregarded the wisdom of many of the saints who understood that listening, rather than speaking to God, is the ultimate act of my reasoning and will. Why do we so highly regard our own deepest thoughts and feelings and so casually disregard God's?

My distorted view of prayer created tremendous resentment and disappointment. From my experiences with other can-do leaders, I had come to expect that when I presented a problem to God, he'd get busy working on a solution. If I posed God a question, God would come up with an answer. If I moved diagonally, then God would move in response, like we were playing a game of checkers. When it didn't work out this way, I began wondering, *Does God hear me? Does God really care? Am I speaking words into thin air?*

Again I struggled with my paradoxical nature. I said I wanted to hear what God had to say, yet I took no time to listen. The sense that I was not getting what I asked for made me wonder if I had said the wrong kind of prayers or the right kind of prayers the wrong way. For me, prayer was like a recipe. Maybe I had failed to add enough baking soda, and that's why the cake didn't rise. So why bother praying if I was missing some crucial—but secret—word or posture that guaranteed the results I wanted? I already had more to do than I could possibly handle. And loneliness, frustration, and disappointment were easier to tolerate than speaking to a God who appeared to be enjoying a game of hide-and-seek at my expense. If God didn't have time to answer my prayers, then I didn't have time to keep praying.

Another misconception that sabotaged prayer was my thinking about God in light of intellectual discoveries I had made. I came to view God as a riddle to be solved or a puzzle with a missing piece I needed to find rather than as a friend to be known and enjoyed. With that assumption coloring my prayer life, it's not surprising that prayer became an exhausting assignment. With all the other things I felt compelled to do, decoding God became just another burdensome obligation. Prayer wore me out.

So I stopped praying. That is, until the next crisis occurred, causing me to again crank up my prayer engines. Unless a crisis loomed, though, I found satisfaction in the many things I felt competent to do. I didn't have enough energy for a life of prayer that taxed my mind and left me feeling tired and disappointed.

Prayer Is Always a Gift

When the followers of Jesus asked for a lesson on prayer, he didn't start a how-to class, he started praying. Prayer is always a gift—a gift we are given, not an accomplishment we take credit for. Even the *desire* to pray is a gift from a loving God. God offers us infinite freedom in determining how to pray. It's wiser to allow our yearning for God to lead us to an approach to communing with God that is the most authentic, effective, and meaningful for each of us.

The wisdom of Teresa of Avila, the Spanish nun whose sufferings gave way to a deep spiritual life and significant service to God and others, is the source of considerable help. Hanging on a wall in one of the rooms at Avila Retreat Center in North Carolina is a tapestry with her words, which suggest I should not become discouraged with my efforts or in my desire to learn how to pray. She says, "Although you meditate, try your hardest, and shed tears, you cannot make this water flow. God is the only one who gives it, and he gives it to whomever he chooses and often, when one is least thinking about it." In other words, prayer is God's business, and what is most necessary is my willingness to surrender to what God desires, trusting God with the results (apparent or otherwise). If I am wise, I'll wait on God and persist in prayer without becoming consumed or frustrated with thinking about what I might receive in return.

The beloved fifteenth-century monk and monastery kitchen worker Brother Lawrence, best known for the way he communed with God in the simple chores of his daily life, acknowledged a time when he felt he had become a failure at prayer. Then one day it occurred to him that he'd always been and would always be a failure at prayer, and from that point he sensed he was making progress. I can relate.

Much of my struggle with prayer is due to teaching I received years ago on how to pray, as though there were one foolproof technique that works best for everyone. Poet Sam Walter Foss, a nineteenth-century New Hampshire journalist, provides a wonderfully tongue-in-cheek critique of people who would tell us that the right way to pray is to "do it like I do!"

> "The proper way for a man to pray," said Deacon Lemuel
>   Keyes;
> "And the only proper attitude is down upon his knees."

> "Nay, I should say the way to pray," said Reverend Doctor
>   Wise,
> "Is standing straight with outstretched arms with shining
>   upturned eyes."

"Oh, no, no, no," said Elder Snow, "such posture is too proud.
A man should pray with eyes fast-closed and head contritely
    bowed."

"It seems to me his hands should be austerely clasped in front
with both thumbs pointing to the ground," said Reverend
    Doctor Blunt.

"Last year I fell in Hodgkin's well head-first," said layman
    Cyrus Brown.
"With both my heels a-stickin' up, my head a-pointin' down;
and I made a prayer right then and there; best prayer I ever said,
the prayin'est prayer I ever prayed, a-standin' on my head."[1]

When I consider all the books, tapes, sermons, and workshops I
have given my attention to concerning prayer, what has been most
helpful is the sage wisdom of Benedictine author Dom Chapman,
who says, "Pray as you can, not as you cannot."[2]

Years ago I attended a seminar on private prayer led by a pastor and
spiritual director I deeply respect. Carefully outlining his "personal rule
for prayer," I left determined to duplicate his experience. If it was the
last thing I ever did, I was going to remain faithful for the remainder
of my life to the same routine. Weeks later, after doing everything I
knew to do to be consistent in my daily times of prayer, I had failed
miserably. Why could I not keep this rule? Finally I embraced wisdom
I had heard before, that the rule you can't keep just might be *someone
else's* rule but not yours. I needed to find my own way.

MINDLESS BUT NOT HEARTLESS

The crisis in my prayer life was the natural consequence of my mind's
being filled with ideas about God, some of them distorted, while my
heart felt far removed from him. In the midst of my disappointment,

God was helping me to discover that real prayer comes from deep within the heart—where the Scriptures say the spirit of Jesus resides. "Because you are children, God has sent the Spirit of his Son into our hearts" (Galatians 4:6). I don't believe there has been the beginning of a discovery that has been more important than this: True prayer takes place in the heart, not in the head. When I am praying I move from my head, where my knowledge of God resides, down into my heart, where my spirit meets God's Spirit.

God clearly longs to commune with us heart to heart. I recall the feelings expressed by the two followers of Jesus who walked with him on the road to Emmaus without recognizing him. But when they learned that it was the resurrected Jesus, they said to each other, "Were not our hearts burning within us while he was talking to us on the road" (Luke 24:32). Jean-Nicholas Grou says, "It is the heart that prays, it is to the heart that God listens and it is the heart that he answers."[3]

A few years ago I was speaking at a high school retreat. Halfway through the event, my son Lee, then eight, asked, "Dad, what are you going to tell them next?" After I gave him a brief summary of my talk, my son replied with a less-than-approving look, "I think you should tell them how to pray."

"Lee," I asked, "how would you suggest I tell them to pray?" In a few moments he replied, "Dad, do you remember how I used to pray...how I used to just tell God things?" (Lucie and I had, in fact, noticed a change in our son's prayers.) "Well, I don't pray that way anymore...that is, from my head. Now I tell God about what's in my heart, then I listen to see if I can hear God tell me what's in his heart."

The thing I've continued learning from Lee and other saints is that praying from the heart may be "mindless" prayer but it's not "heartless" prayer. This kind of prayer requires that I descend from my mind into my heart where I come face to face with the living Lord who knows me and who still loves me beyond my wildest dreams.

When I pray from my heart, there's no hiding or playing games. Instead, my heart is exposed to the Presence within, and my prayer becomes more a way of being with God than an act of doing something for God. Prayer from my heart rises from the core of who I am as a person and shapes the whole of my existence and my relationship with God. Prayer becomes an experience of living in the mystery and wonder of God's embrace.

As I offer my prayers from the recesses of my heart, I hear more clearly the whispering voice of God. In George Bernard Shaw's play *Saint Joan*, Charles, king of France, complains to Joan of Arc that God spoke to her, a peasant girl, but not to him. But Joan wisely corrected King Charles: "The voices do come to you, but you do not hear them. When the angelus rings you cross yourself and have done with it; but if you prayed from your heart, and listened...you would hear the voices as well as I do."[4] As God gives us grace to pray from our heart, we are placed in an attentive and listening posture.

Every August I spend a long weekend with a group of men who come from various walks of life. We call ourselves The Notorious Sinners, and every indication suggests we're living up to our name. We tell each other the truth about what's in our heart, its delights and its difficulties. And we listen. We tell of our troubles, joys, yearnings, failures, dislikes, and temptations. And we listen. We expose our wounds, our indifference to what's good, our interest in what's evil, and our volatility. And we listen.

I've told these men how self-love has made me unjust to others, how self-hatred has kept me from knowing the love of God and others, and how pride has disguised me to others and to myself. And they have listened. This experience of exposing my life, more than any other situation, has opened me to the kind of prayer for which my heart has always yearned. As I've continued learning to be vulnerable in the company of these men, I've also continued learning to be more vulnerable with God. As I continue to pray from my heart, my very nature has begun to change, because prayer has opened the eyes of my soul to the deepest truth about God and me.

The Notorious Sinners met without me last summer. Due to a family crisis, I had to cancel my plans to attend. Several weeks later as I was traveling late at night and far from home, I was attacked by a bout of loneliness. I prayed to know God's nearness, but nothing changed. Remembering Jesus' words "where two or three are gathered in my name, I am there among them" (Matthew 18:20), I called one of the guys in the group and asked if we could visit on the phone. I began to express the deep loneliness and sadness I was feeling. I couldn't explain the depth or severity of this feeling—I don't understand it to this day. But I told my friend this was no ordinary, fleeting brush with melancholy. I revealed to him my deepest fear and doubt, and I admitted that although I had given no thought to taking my life, it was easy for me to wish I could die.

"I don't know how much longer I can live with this pain," I finally said. Having told all I could, I waited to hear the consoling words I felt certain he would offer. However, no words came. For a moment, I wondered if we'd been disconnected. Then I heard him sniffle and clear his throat. "Fil, God and I love you, and neither of us is going to leave you."

DISCOVERING HOW TO PRAY

Knowing I needed a regular exercise plan to improve my health, for years I tried to find something I could enjoy enough to do regularly. At first I tried what I saw most others doing: running. The only problem was I hated running! Even my most enjoyable run was terrible drudgery.

Then a friend gave me an article that suggested walking might provide the same benefit as running without as many negative side effects. So swallowing my macho pride, late one evening I drove to a neighborhood where I knew no one. I donned a baseball cap (I almost wore dark glasses) and tried doing what I believed only sissies and old men do…I began walking. It wasn't long before I made a surprising discovery. I loved walking! Today it's still my favorite form of exercise.

In both exercise and prayer, an effective way to identify the most meaningful practice is to pay attention to the things that have been meaningful in the past. Perhaps prayer was richest when you were walking in a park, sitting in a quiet corner of your home, walking through the woods or along the shoreline, or kneeling in a chapel. If a particular form of prayer brought you to a meaningful encounter with God in the past, it might be one of your best ways to pray today.

A few years ago while guiding a silent retreat, I met privately with an agitated retreat participant. "Why does this have to be so difficult?" he asked. "It seems God is playing games. I'm trying hard to connect with God, but nothing seems to be working. I wish God cared about my feelings as much as I do."

After listening for a while longer, I gently asked, "Do you recall a time when you enjoyed a particular sense of God's presence and felt connected to the One your soul thirsts for now?" He began smiling and seemed to calm down as he recalled an afternoon, when walking alone through the woods, he was overcome by a sense of God's nearness and affection.

"How have you spent your time so far at this retreat?" I asked.

"I've spent most of it sitting in that dumb chapel thinking that's where I should try to pray."

"Perhaps you'd be wise to leave the chapel and take a walk in the woods," I suggested. With a smile, he agreed.

That evening as he was leaving dinner he handed me a note. "God and I had a fantastic time in the woods this afternoon. Thanks for the helpful advice!"

Several years ago I scheduled some time for my own personal solitude retreat. The setting was a Spartan cabin in the middle of a forest.

After settling in, I set out to pray. I've come to expect to feel distance from God, at least initially. But this time the distance lasted. The more determined I became to connect with God, the farther I felt I was drifting. Finally, after hours of restless trying, I decided to do something I felt confident I could achieve. Like a little child, pouting because things didn't go his way, I climbed into the cabin's loft to take a nap, the spiritual equivalent of picking up my marbles and going home. As I crawled between the covers and listened to the rain on the tin roof overhead, my body began to relax. By this time I had forgotten about trying to pray. All I had on my mind was taking a nap. As I lay there, a wave of gratitude for this comfortable, safe, and quiet place began to engulf me. I felt so full of peace. Before I realized what was happening, I began thanking God for the rain and the rest and the closeness to God that I felt.

We've all experienced the situation where the harder we try to do something the worse the results. I was beginning to learn that, for me, prayer is something that doesn't improve with clench-jawed effort.

A MODEL PRAYER

Prior to offering his friends a model prayer known today as the Lord's Prayer, Jesus spoke these words:

> Here's what I want you to do: Find a quiet, secluded place so
> you won't be tempted to role-play before God. Just be there as
> simply and honestly as you can manage. The focus will shift
> from you to God, and you will begin to sense His grace.
> (Matthew 6:6, MSG)

We would be foolish to ignore Jesus' straightforward wisdom. He eliminates any doubt about whether he wants us to pray by simply saying, "Here's what I want you to do." Immediately following this affirmation, he focuses on the importance of where I pray. I don't believe he is saying there are places where prayer *cannot* occur. However, the setting can be an enormous help or hindrance. My wife and I can talk anywhere. However, there are times when it helps to be attentive to the setting when we intend to spend time with each other. *Cozy, intimate, quiet, removed,* and *comfortable* are words that come to mind when considering the ideal setting for getting away together.

Not too long ago, while sharing a quiet evening together, Lucie made the comment, "Sometime soon I'd like for you to take me away." Admittedly, I was a bit suspicious. "Is something wrong?" To which she playfully replied, "Not yet."

In both my relationships with Lucie and God, I have discovered the priceless value of withdrawing from the company of others. With Lucie and with God, creating an atmosphere that supports our purpose together has been helpful. By taking care with the setting, I affirm, "You are all that matters to me."

Beyond the setting, it's important to consider the form of prayer and the substance it reflects. Openness and vulnerability are crucial. (Whom do we think we're fooling when we put up a front for Jesus?) Jesus urges me to be there, as simply and honestly as I can manage. But sometimes the simple act of "being there" in the moment is the greatest challenge. So much of my life is focused either on the past or the future. We must be present in the moment, because that's where God is. Only the memory of God is in the past, and all I can do about the future is trust that God will meet me there when the future becomes the present. God chooses to be found in the present.

Ceaseless prayer is not about a constant flow of words, focused thoughts, or enduring feelings toward God. Instead, it's a simple practice of keeping company with the God who is always present and attentive to us. Just as Saint Francis of Assisi is quoted as saying, "We preach Jesus Christ, and when necessary we use words," I was beginning to understand that there are times when words or even my focused attention are not necessary for prayer to occur. A German proverb says, "The fewer the words, the better the prayer." Sometimes words become a distraction. Short, simple prayers often nurture the deepest and most heartfelt needs in my life.

Sometime ago my spiritual director encouraged me to ask God for a prayer that could companion me along the way. I followed the advice, and God led me to the words "I'm your special son." This was fitting when considering one of my greatest struggles has been accepting God's acceptance of me. Perhaps this has its origin in my struggle to gain and experience my birth father's love and approval. Unresolved issues with our parents often are projected onto our view of God. The quiet and gentle repetition of this prayer has, at times, ushered in a deeper and more abiding awareness of God's tender love and acceptance. Far from a magic formula or an attempt to manipulate God, these words help me focus, move from my head into my heart, and open space for God to work. Faithfulness to this simple prayer has led to an experience of rest and opened me to God's transforming presence.

Such prayers are highly portable—they easily accompany us throughout the day. Simple prayers such as this one can and should be woven into the fabric of our lives.

Learning to Pray by Praying

Just as it's easiest to learn a foreign language when we are forced to speak it, we learn the most about how to pray when we're praying. Responding to a question about the best form of prayer, a wise saint, George Buttrick, said, "There is no rule of thumb, for the reason that every thumbprint is different and distinct."[5] There are as many ways to pray as there are moments in a day. And every moment is a moment for some kind of praying. This truth will set us free as we continue to pray as we can, not as we can't.

The Scriptures chronicle an endless variety of forms and styles and approaches to prayer. Perhaps these prayers reflect the culture. Perhaps they reflect the uniqueness of the individual. Or perhaps they all reflect the mystery, wonder, and vastness of God. Jeremiah stood before God as he offered prayers for his people. Nehemiah sat down when he prayed. Abraham was on his face while praying. Daniel prayed three times a day at a set time and in a set place. Ezekiel prayed with a loud voice. Hannah prayed without words. Moses spent much time listening to God. A blind beggar offered a brief appeal. Peter prayed on his knees and when he was sinking. Paul prayed in the spirit. David prayed in the morning and spontaneously throughout the day and night. Job cried out to God in pain, anger, and despair. Mary called out in gladness and ecstasy. Jonah prayed from the belly of a fish. Anna prayed night and day in the temple.[6] Other saints mentioned in the Scriptures offered prayers in sacred places and on secular streets. Some prayed with the language of angels while others stuttered and stammered. Some prayed wearing priestly ceremonial dress, others in sackcloth and ashes. And at least one, a king, took off his clothes and danced.

Walking, wobbling, or wallowing, standing, kneeling, or dancing, they came and offered their prayers. Speaking their own words, or without any words, they offered their prayers. Raising their hands, clenching their fists, or clasping their hands in humility, they prayed. With full or empty stomachs, with full or empty hearts, they spoke to God.

These saints didn't teach us a specific form for prayer; they taught us to pray.

SERIOUS IMPLICATIONS

At the time I began writing this chapter on prayer, I visited an elderly friend who was feeling slight ill effects from his annual flu vaccination. He had been given a small dose of the flu virus in order to activate his body's immune system, thus protecting him from the life-threatening virus. In the same way, could casual exposure to prayer "protect" me from the real thing? For years I began my day hurriedly praying brief prayers and then going away thinking, "There, that's enough. I've prayed." Before I knew what had happened, I was drawn into a whirlwind of activity that left no space in my life for ongoing communion with God. A little prayer had kept me away from true prayer.

In recent years I've begun to understand that prayer is more "gift given" than "mission accomplished." Out of his love for me, Jesus makes me the object of his attention and his affection. Out of my love for him, Jesus becomes the object of my attention and affection. Focusing on Jesus is more helpful than placing all of my attention on praying in a particular way. If I am not faithful to the discipline of prayer, in whatever form, bit by bit I will forget God. I must beg God daily for the grace to live a life of unceasing prayer. I must regularly spend time with God speaking and listening, pondering and getting to know God. If I do anything but this, my mind and my heart will be consumed with other interests and concerns. Before long I will fail to recognize the sound of God's voice, and I will stop speaking to God. I know this from hard experience.

Thirty years ago when I began working for a Christian ministry to teenagers, I can remember saying to God, "I'm sorry I have so little time, if any, to be alone with you, but the demands of my ministry are so great and the needs of the students are so extreme, I simply can't afford more time." After offering the same excuse countless times, I less frequently expressed any sadness or regret over neglected prayer and feverishly went on with my work. Days would pass without any prayer, and it finally became clear: This is not love. Love always calls for communication and a longing to share life with the One who is the object of our affection.

When I became ruthlessly honest about my prayerless life, I had to admit if I were a lover of God, I would find a way to be with my Beloved. This clarity about my relationship with God was a dreadfully painful reality, and yet recognizing it has proven to be an invaluable gift. One of the keys to arresting the destructive pace of my life has been to see the value of establishing a simple rule for ceaseless prayer and then praying.

—POINTS TO PONDER—

1. How much freedom do you feel to explore the many ways there are to pray? Is there a voice in the back of your head that insists you must pray a certain way?
2. What forms of prayer are most natural and meaningful to you? Which ones seem to rob you of motivation?
3. What aspect of your relationship with God does the most to encourage you to pray?
4. What are the things that fill your life and prevent you from being silent and listening to God?
5. How open and honest is your prayer? Do you find it difficult to be yourself with God? Do you find yourself trying to hide things from him?

SACRED SCRIPTURE

Immersing Your Life in God's Revelation

When you read God's word, you must constantly be saying
to yourself, "It is talking to me, and about me."

—Søren Kierkegaard

Several years have passed since a dear friend laid me bare with a penetrating observation. "Fil," he said, "you are all the time quoting authors who have influenced your life…but you rarely mention the Bible." His truthful words hurt, and even today I feel their sting. But along with sadness and shame came eventual healing.

What broke my heart was the realization that I was more interested in what the Scriptures had spoken to others than in hearing what the Scriptures would say to me. I wasn't giving God a chance to speak directly to me. I suspected I'd been guarding my life against the reforming words of Scripture, but I wasn't certain why. That night, through my friend, I heard the clear call for change.

I typically would read the Bible every day, but I figuratively held it at arm's length. God was about to open my eyes to the motives that had driven my sloppy approach to reading God's sacred Word.

In a letter to his youngest sister, Vincent van Gogh wrote, "[Y]ou…read books…to draw from them the energy to act."[1] The first time I read those words I wondered, *Have I been reading the*

Scriptures the way van Gogh's sister read books? Am I simply looking for pointers from God on how to improve my efficiency in ministry?

I had taken a pragmatic and ultimately neurotic approach to God's holy words. I had read the Scriptures looking for facts and information so I could impress others with my knowledge and understanding. I had read the Scriptures looking for "Bible Bullets" that I could use to protect myself and wound others when they attacked my plans or beliefs. I had read the Scriptures looking for principles to assist me in becoming more successful. I had read the Scriptures looking for promises to help me feel safe and secure. I had read the Scriptures looking for inspiration and stories so that when I spoke to a crowd I would be affirmed as a gifted communicator.[2]

Bottom line, I had read the Scriptures looking for anything that might support my own interests and desires and would allow me to live in the illusion that I was in control. I had become frighteningly like the Pharisees who were, in fact, the best Bible students of the first century, yet in the process they missed out on knowing Jesus. Jesus read them accurately when he said, "You search the scriptures because you think that in them you have eternal life.… Yet you refuse to come to me to have life" (John 5:39-40). Like the Pharisees, I was more interested in security than intimacy.

Van Gogh concluded his letter by explaining, "I…read books to find the artist who wrote them."[3] In my reading of the Word of God, I had failed to recognize God and to be embraced by God's Word. However, that was beginning to change. I was on the path to discovering that the Scriptures reveal a Person who is tirelessly searching for me with a Lover's intensity. I was beginning to understand that Jesus is a Person who wants not simply a personal relationship with me but an intimate one.

The Word of God is not a self-help book nor a placebo to calm our fears. Neither is it a guide to career success or greater effectiveness in ministry. It is, in truth, a love letter that invites us to be embraced by the Lover who wrote the letter. Sacred Scripture has tremendous power to free us from the mold the world squeezes us into. The God of the universe, who, in the beginning, shaped life into existence with spoken words, today speaks words meant to reshape our lives.

For this reshaping power to take effect, I had to begin reading the words slowly, carefully, and prayerfully, leaving room enough for me to hear God whisper, "Stay with me, Fil. Pay attention to me. Hear my words of affection. Don't be in such a hurry." Real reading includes hearing, and hearing God's words is essential in recovering our lives from the soul-killing addictions to noise, performance, and activity.

A New Way to Read

I need an antivenin, but which one will counteract the poison of this absurdly busy and demanding world? How can I resist the pull toward a maddening pace that threatens my soul's love relationship with God? The wisdom of the sacred Scriptures and the saints who read them suggests that the answer, at least in part, centers not on just our read-ing of the Word of God, but *how* we read the Word of God. Reading the Bible prayerfully does at least two profound things: It tells me who I am and what I bring to the Word of God, and it tells me who God is and what the Word of God brings to me. Spiritual reading doesn't include hearing; spiritual reading *is* hearing. This kind of reading demonstrates my desire for God to come closer to me and to reshape my life.

In 1677 Henry Scougal offered the following insight in his book *The Life of God in the Soul of Man:* "The worth and excellency of a soul is to be measured by the object of its love."[4] My soul has known fail-ure, disappointment, and shame because of its suffocating attachments to influence, recognition, and busyness. But in recent years, as my soul has been seized by the power of God's unbridled affection, I have slowly (and painfully) seen a change in the object of my soul's affection.

There is a story about a young boy who lived in a quaint mountain village. Just outside the village was a quiet knoll where he'd often go to sit and gaze at a peculiar rock formation. As if carved into the side of the mountain, the rocks bore the distinct likeness of an old man. As the boy entered the teen years, he maintained his habit of returning to this spot to stare at the image. Even as a young man, despite the responsibility of a family and other obligations, he continued the habit. Finally, as an elderly man, with much less to occupy his time, he would return to his safe haven and sit for hours, simply gazing at the likeness of the old man on the side of the mountain. One day, while walking through the village, a tourist stopped the man and asked him, "Did anyone ever tell you that you look like the face on the side of the mountain?"

I have lived long enough to know that whatever (and whomever) I most love will do the most to shape my life. I will take on the likeness of the object of my affection. If I love recognition most, my longing for significance will shape me. If I love money, my yearning for more assets will shape me. If I love God most, the Father, Son, and Holy Spirit will shape me in their image.

Scripture affirms this profound reality on almost every page. Hosea, the Old Testament prophet, reported that the people of Israel "became detestable like the thing they loved" (Hosea 9:10). Yet Jesus, who never wavered or turned from his love and devotion to his Abba, "grew and became strong, filled with wisdom; and the favor of God was upon him" (Luke 2:40).

The author of Psalm 119, whose affection was set fully on God, was passionately devoted to the Word of God. This poet was humble in acknowledging his or her own wayward behavior and knew the pain (and benefits) of God's correction. Speaking from a deep reservoir of hard-won insights, the psalmist asked and answered a crucial question:

How can a young person live a clean life?
> By carefully reading the map of your Word.

I'm single-minded in pursuit of you;
> don't let me miss the road signs you've posted.

I've banked your promises in the vault of my heart
> so I won't sin myself bankrupt....

I ponder every morsel of wisdom from you....

I relish everything you've told me of life,
> I won't forget a word of it....

I cherish your commandments—oh, how I love them!—
> relishing every fragment of your counsel....

By your words I can see where I'm going;
> they throw a beam of light on my dark path.
> (Psalm 119:9-11,15-16,47-48,105, MSG)

Learning to read the Scriptures in a way that is life forming is learning to listen. By listening as I read Scripture, I have found myself remaining with the words and their remaining with me for much longer periods than before.

I remember my grandfather sitting on a bench beneath a tall, longleaf pine in front of his home. He spent a good bit of his time on that bench, and most of it with a plug of Beechnut tucked in one side of his cheek. One day as we sat there, I asked, "Granddaddy, why do you keep that plug of tobacco in your mouth?" Slowly shifting it from one cheek to the other, he replied, "I reckon it just keeps me company."

Like Granddaddy with his plug of tobacco, most of us keep company with something on our minds. Whatever these things are—worries, fears, doubts, anger, confusion, disappointment, or dread—they have a way of giving shape to our lives. Sadly, some things and some thoughts make bad company. That's why it's so important to keep open spaces in our lives when we listen to the Word of God.

THE PRACTICE OF SPIRITUAL READING

Reading the Word with openness to God is risky business. I have seen it lead to dramatic changes.

For years I've lived with chronic lower-back pain. I've tried countless treatments and exercises. Several years ago a friend came to our home with a large brown medicine bottle bearing no label. I should have been wary, but my friend boldly asserted that I would soon be thanking him for this long-awaited cure. "All you do is rub it twice a day on the area that hurts, and before you know it, you'll be feeling as good as new," he explained. "Oh, and one more thing…you'll know it's beginning to work when your breath starts to stink."

I was foolish enough to try it, and as promised, in a few days my breath smelled atrocious. My body had absorbed this pungent potion to the point that my breath was changed. Sadly, however, the unlabeled horse liniment failed to help my back. In contrast, when I allow the Word of God to be absorbed into my heart and mind and to work its way into my life, its effects are noticeable, and the changes it brings—always—are positive.

The leader of the Protestant Reformation, Martin Luther, whose life was profoundly changed by the thoughtful reading of Scripture, said, "The Bible is alive, it speaks to me, it has feet, it runs after me; it has hands, it lays hold of me."[5] Of all the things chasing after me and clamoring for my devotion, my life is most secure when I allow my affection to be apprehended by God's wisdom and care for me, expressed in the sacred Scriptures.

Long lines of people have lived in reliance on the wisdom of God's counsel, and they continue to encourage us to follow their path. The words of Theonas of Alexandria, who lived centuries ago, still echoes this appeal: "Let no day pass by without reading some portion of the sacred scriptures and giving some space to meditation; for nothing feeds the soul so well as those sacred studies do."[6] The wisdom of the ages reveals there's no more reliable source of information for my transformation than the sacred Scriptures.

With that settled, the next question is, how can we read the Scriptures in such a way that it will shape our lives? The answer is to practice spiritual reading.

The monks of Mepkin Abbey introduced me to spiritual reading. They begin and end their days with hearing the Word of God. Seven times a day the monks gather to say or sing the psalms, the church's language of prayer from ancient times, and to meditate on Scripture. In between these community times, they carry the Word within them or, at times, the Word carries them. These sacred words chart the natural features of the human experience: love and hate, harmony and conflict, rest and struggle, loyalty and betrayal, presence and absence, the space between what is anticipated and what actually occurs. In each of these common places, the monks search for signs of the presence and activity of God. Their purpose is to offer thanks for what has been given and to have their lives enveloped in the Word of God.

Life-enriching words, ebbing and flowing around and through their lives, purify, calm, enliven, and sometimes flood the souls of these holy men. Over the course of a lifetime, a monk learns the cadence of the Word, comes to know the words of the Word by heart, and is shaped by the Word. The sacred Word is chewed, savored, swallowed, digested ever so slowly. For these monks the sacred Word tastes of life, the taste of God.

The words of God's Word work together to form the message of transformation. My soul is enriched when, instead of taking the words apart, I bring them together in my deepest parts. Instead of debating whether I agree or disagree, I think about which words God is speaking directly to me. Instead of looking for information that I can use to impress or inspire others, I let a word penetrate into hidden places in my heart. Then and only then is my soul truly shaped by the Word.

Spiritual reading invites me into a progression through the four movements of reading, meditating, praying, and contemplating.

READING FOR TRANSFORMATION *(Lectio)*

Reading possesses the power to entertain, inspire, inform, and to help us discover and apply truth to our lives. Yet not all reading—even the reading of Scripture—is the same. There is reading for information and reading for transformation. When I'm reading the Scriptures for information, I approach the text as an object to be studied and understood. It becomes something I am trying to grasp or comprehend. I look for the factual, the useful, the relevant. But when I read for transformation, I am no longer working on the text. Instead, I am inviting the text to work on me. Rather than picking the words apart, I allow them to come together in the deepest part of my being. A friend of mine says, "Don't just read the Bible, let the Bible read you." This approach focuses on the dynamics of change that reshape my life.

There exists a need for both approaches. However, when I recall how I was first taught to read the Scriptures, it was limited to searching for precepts and principles rather than opening me to an encounter with God. As I searched for useful facts, I was always in control. The introduction of *lectio divina* has begun to correct this imbalance, shifting the control from me to God and his Spirit.[7]

If I am seeking information while reading the story of the woman breaking the alabaster jar of perfume and pouring it on Jesus' head (Mark 14:3-9), I may ask, "Did this really happen? Who is telling this story and why should I believe him? And what in the world is alabaster?" But when I read the same story with spiritual alertness, allowing the words to call me to prayer and contemplation, something quite different occurs. When I invite God to shape my life as I read transformationally, new and different kinds of questions emerge. What life experience led this woman to so boldly offer this gift? What is God saying to me about my life and how I might be more extravagant in expressing my love? How do others' reactions to my affection for God affect me?

When I read the Scriptures in this way, I begin by choosing a relatively brief passage, and I read it slowly. I relax. When possible, I read aloud. Something about hearing the words helps me internalize them. As I slow down, I invite God to wander through the passage with me. I resist the tendency to be concerned about insights, discoveries, or understanding. What's important is that I simply pay attention to what is happening.

One of the greatest challenges we encounter in spiritual reading is knowing how to live with mystery and how to feel comfortable with not knowing. We need to learn how "not to know." This involves the call to humility and to live more comfortably with mystery. Given my earlier training, this is difficult. After all, I was taught to bring every resource to bear to enhance understanding and to leave no room for mystery. I was trained to press through until there was some insight or understanding. The burden was on me to analyze the text until I found the key to transformation.

Now I hear the call to walk through the words of sacred Scripture more aware of the Author's presence, listening for God's voice and trusting God to clarify, point to, and illuminate those things that are not yet understood. God is responsible for the outcome and must remain in charge. My role is not to always know or understand but to trust. Ultimately the important result is being formed rather than informed. The practical wisdom and insight of Thomas à Kempis is helpful when he says, "Our own curiosity often hinders us in reading the Scriptures, because we wish to understand and argue when we should read on with humility, simplicity and faith."[8]

MEDITATION *(Meditatio)*

One day I was enjoying a hot dog at my favorite stand when I spilled a big glob of mustard on my sweater. Rather than hastily wiping it off, I slowly and carefully began to remove it. In a matter of a few minutes, I successfully fulfilled my mission without leaving a trace of the stain. I was so proud! In that same moment, I believe God spoke to me: "Fil, that is exactly what you do with my Word. Rather than allow it to remain with you and work its way into your life, you find a way to insulate yourself from what I'm saying. You remove it…you don't let it soak in. You refuse to let it re-form you! Fil, if you'll let me, I want to 'mark' your life with my love."

God wants the Word to give form and substance to my life. God is far more interested in the Word's getting through to me than my getting through the Word. What I know is not nearly as important as the impact of knowledge on my life. As such, one path that leads to positive change is meditation on Scripture. As I move from reading to meditation, I begin to saturate and immerse myself in the Word, I let God in, and I let God detain me. In meditation I want to penetrate the Scriptures until they are given an opportunity to penetrate me. There is no anxious rush to get to the next verse. How much I read is not important. How deeply I read is. As one of the saints suggested, "If you read quickly it will benefit you little. You will be like a bee that merely skims the surface of a flower."[9] When meditating on the Word, I try to linger and plunge myself into the words so as to receive "its deepest nectar."

Over many years Lucie and I have had numerous friends live in our home. One friend had a most uncommon habit. He would eat his food ever so slowly, chewing and chewing and chewing and chewing and chewing. Occasionally, he would place the well-chewed food in his cheek and converse for a while, then return to his chewing.

One evening I could resist the urge no longer. "Why do you do this?" I asked. "Why this forever chewing of your food?" With a hint of a smile, he shifted his food to his cheek and replied, "I love the taste of food. I have never understood why anyone would want to swallow something that tastes so good while it still has its flavor, so I chew until the flavor is gone."

His words remind me of those spoken by God when he commissioned Joshua to establish Israel in the promised land: "This book of the law shall not depart out of your mouth; you shall meditate on it day and night, so that you may be careful to act in accordance with all that is written in it. For then you shall make your way prosperous, and then you shall be successful" (Joshua 1:8). I blush with embarrassment when I recall some of the outrageous plans I adopted for prosperity and success that instead led to disappointment and frustration. Meditating on the Word of God brings true prosperity.

When meditating on a brief passage, I narrow my focus to the words or phrases that have captured my attention. I was walking through a garden once and picked a particularly beautiful flower. The fragrance was so sweet that after I had put the flower in a vase, I could still detect its fragrance on my fingers hours later. The same is true with the sacred Scriptures. Sometimes a word or phrase is so useful, so inspiring or beautiful that I find I can't escape it; I must stay with the word. I invite the word to come with me through the day. I invite the word to shape me, to add the quality it represents to my life.

I have also found it helpful to call upon all five senses when meditating on biblical stories. This enlivens the stories and helps in the transition from the cognitive, analytical stage to the affective, feeling stage of my being. For example, for months I've remained with the story of the woman who brought the alabaster jar and anointed Jesus' head with the perfume. With my imagination, I have been able to see, hear, smell, feel, and taste the entire experience.

I have also found it helpful to place myself in the story as a character or inanimate object. Referring again to the story of anointing, I have imagined being Jesus, the woman, Simon the leper, a waiter, the jar, the perfume, and the woman's hands. As part of my meditation, I have sometimes written a narrative account of my experience as that person or object. These exercises are profoundly meaningful, at times in ways I don't fully understand. But my intuition says the Word is shaping me.

I have meditated on a particular story in Scripture while taking a walk, drawing pictures or images, working with modeling clay, and writing down the words that stand out. It always seems to take more time than I feel I have, but it has become something I must do, that is, if I am to cease from being this driven and outrageously busy person always striving to achieve. The one thing I really want to achieve is the love of God, and his love is achieved through nothing other than my reaching out and accepting it.

I won't speculate on how these exercises have changed my life. And besides, how they have affected me will not be exactly how they affect you. My meditations on the story of the woman who poured her perfume all over Jesus has elevated the affections of my heart toward Jesus. Just like the woman in the story, I long to be passionately indifferent to the reactions of those around me, lost in the extravagant expression of my affection for Jesus. I want my love for God to become as wild, reckless, and free as his for me.

Often I fall victim to distractions and daydreaming. As Thomas Merton expressed in *New Seeds of Contemplation,* "It is much better to desire God without being able to think clearly of Him, than to have marvelous thoughts about Him without desiring to enter into union with His will."[10] I find that the gentler I am in my response to my distractions, the better. I like to think of distractions as having a quality like that of my children when they were little, who meant no harm when they interrupted. However, whenever I tried to ignore them or told them harshly to go away, they persisted in their efforts to gain my attention. Yet often when I explained that I was busy at the moment but wanted to give them my undivided attention later that day, their waiting became easier.

PRAYER *(Oratio)*

I have a friend who teaches a series of Bible studies that includes one concerning the responsibility of God's people toward the poor. One day after this man presented the lesson, he prayed for those he'd instructed that God would penetrate their lives with the truth. As he prayed for them, God penetrated his heart with a question, "Who that is poor do you care for?" My friend painfully acknowledged he didn't know anyone who was poor. I believe his response was really a prayer, specifically associated with the hours he had spent reading and meditating on God's Word.

Immediately he called a local group that offers assistance to at-risk kids and expressed his interest in being connected to one of the children in their program. Today my white, upper-middle-class bachelor friend is the father of an adopted African American son whose life had previously been greatly troubled. Initially, this man assumed the life of the child would be the life most affected and enriched. Today, however, he would say that the impact on his own life has been most profound. The Word of God has clearly shaped my friend's life!

The movement from meditation to prayer may be subtle or even unnoticed, nonetheless, it is the response of my heart to what has been occupying and preoccupying my mind. It carries me from hearing the truth that God has spoken to me to its implications for my life, from understanding to obeying. Depending on how the "living and active" Word is treating me (see Hebrews 4:12), the experience of prayer can be either pleasant and tender or agonizing and revealing. God's Word has a way of cutting through everything and exposing my doubts, defenses, thoughts, and intentions. When my hateful and manipulative tactics are "naked and laid bare to the eyes of the one to whom we must render an account" (Hebrews 4:13), prayer becomes a time for regret, confession, and repentance. Yet at other times when my thoughtful, caring, and compassionate intentions are exposed, prayer becomes a time for joy, gratitude, and celebration. God makes sure I receive whatever I need.

Sometimes I get into the rut of reducing my time for prayer to a method or mindless routine, and I realize the need to slow down and become more attentive to God's presence. Something as simple as lighting a candle has a way of reminding me or calling me back to the awareness of God's presence with me in prayer.

In lectio divina there is a temptation to replace my praying with reading. It is helpful to keep in mind that my reading of and meditation on the passage is the path that leads to a personal response and for listening to what God might wish to say. My time praying is for my heart to respond as I move from my mind to my will. When I take the time to internalize the words I have read, I am invited to embrace the practical consequences of the truth and its implications for my life. Lectio divina is not a regimented, lockstep, sequential progression. During lectio divina, prayer can happen at any moment. Again, God is the One leading and in control.

When I find myself struggling with distractions, I often return to the passage for help in refocusing my attention. Teresa of Avila referred to prayer as a small fire that occasionally needs to be fed a twig to keep burning. A twig is a few words from a passage, and usually a few are all that are needed.

I once was visiting with a therapist who told me some things I badly needed to hear. The words were not pleasant or affirming but necessary. As I listened, I began to feel terribly vulnerable. I became embarrassed as the truth about my self-centered and controlling tendencies began to sink in. I wanted to run and hide. But I stayed. When he finished, he asked me to tell him what I had heard. I didn't want to repeat these things! Hearing *him* say them had been bad enough. But as I began to tell him what I had heard him say, something strange began to happen. The information he had given me that I was now repeating started to grip me. In saying what I had heard, it became much more than facts, data, and information; it became knowledge and truth, truth that became the impetus for change. When I had finished stating what I had heard him say, I asked if I could go on. Without waiting, I added, "I'm sorry for these things. They are true, and I realize I have been blind to them. I don't want to be this kind of person. Will you help me understand what I need to do to change?"

The sacred Scriptures are inspired by God and useful in "showing us truth, exposing our rebellion, correcting our mistakes, training us to live God's way" (2 Timothy 3:16, MSG). When I am deliberate and thoughtful in slowly reading the words of God, taking time to meditate on them, and begin to tell God what I have heard and how it relates to my life, stuff just happens! The information becomes something much more than just data; it becomes knowledge and truth, the impetus for real change.

CONTEMPLATION *(Contemplatio)*

Early this summer I sat on the beach alone with my Bible. After slowly reading a brief passage several times, paying attention to the few words that kept standing out, I began to ponder the words and phrases that had captured my attention. Like a cube of ice slowly melting in my mouth, I let the words settle and dissolve. Again it was the story of the woman who loved Jesus extravagantly. "Why this waste?… Leave her alone.… Why are you bothering her?…a beautiful thing… She did what she could." I was particularly attracted to the words "she did what she could" (Mark 14:8, NIV). I began to feel drawn to meditate on these words. Who was this woman? What had her life consisted of prior to this episode? What was in her heart and mind at this moment?

As I meditated, my imagination came alive. I began to picture the expression on her face. I sensed how detached she was from the crowd's judgmental reaction. I heard the jar break and smelled the perfume. With my mind's eye, I saw the corners of Jesus' mouth turn up as he broke into a wide grin. I saw the perfume running down his hair, all over his well-formed smile, the wrinkles around his mouth, into his beard, soaking his robe. Even more, his eyes smiled with gratitude, like eyes do in that split second before he said, "Thanks, Mary. That's beautiful."

I had intended to pray that morning, and without knowing what was happening, I found myself praying, "Jesus, I want so much to be like her. I wish I were as detached as she seemed to be. It makes me so sad that what others think about me controls me. Jesus, make me more like her. In my heart, I sense that is the person I really am. But it feels like I'm keeping that real me locked up for fear of what my real self might do if ever set free."

After a while I stopped talking. There was nothing more to say. I just rested and listened. I began what I have come to refer to as "the big stare." For the next few minutes, I waited in silence. I felt the same as I had the night before when Lucie, our two sons, and I had gone out on a boat, ridden around for a while, eaten our dinner, talked, and anchored the boat so we could watch the sun set. Everyone sat quietly, watching and waiting…knowing something spectacular was happening, and if we would pay attention, we would get to see it.

It was quieter than the quietest night. The sky was furrowed with wispy bands of altostratus clouds. As the sun began its descent, the color ranged from the most delicate pearl-like pinks to the deepest fiery red. It was so breathtakingly beautiful that I prayed for the gift of memory to recall its transient glory.

The language of contemplation is silence, and the necessary action is unreserved openness. Like the moment before a photographer takes a photograph, when she suddenly says, "Hold it," and everyone stops talking and waits, contemplation starts when I stop talking and listen in simple and loving attentiveness. I take off the sandals of my thoughts, ideas, dreams, and imaginations, and quietly rest and listen on that holy ground.

Once a rural preacher, speaking of this way of reading and "being with" the Scriptures, said, "I read myself full. I think myself clear. I pray myself hot, and I let myself cool." Contemplation is letting myself cool. Contemplation is not primarily an activity of the mind or a state of daydreaming. It is a quality of presence, an openness to what is not seen yet is real.

One of my favorite writers tells the simple story of an older man who had the habit of slipping into a certain chapel at the same time every day. There he would sit and apparently do nothing. The priest observed this silent visitor with growing curiosity. One day, unable to contain his wondering any longer, he asked the old man why he came to the chapel. "What do you do in there?"

The old man, with a kind and loving twinkle in his eye, offered this explanation: "I look at God. God looks at me. And we smile."

Even Thomas Merton, one of the twentieth century's most pro-lific writers about contemplation, acknowledged that contemplation can't be taught or clearly explained: "It can only be hinted at, sug-gested, pointed to, symbolized."[11] It seems that the more scientific and objective our attempts to analyze contemplation, the more we empty it of its substance. Contemplation is beyond the reach of words and rational understanding. Contemplation is nothing more and nothing less than an awareness of the reality of God.

My heart's deepest yearning is that in lectio divina, as I engage in the daily exercise of slowly reading the sacred Scriptures, my mind and heart will be filled with ideas that, in the end, lead my heart to the heart of God. Then someday our two hearts will beat in me as one. Up until now, I've been doing all the talking. Why don't you stop reading, turn the book over, and ask yourself, "What is my deepest longing?"

—POINTS TO PONDER—

1. Considering your schedule, how can you structure your day or week so that regularly reading sacred Scripture is more likely to occur? What might you have to remove from your schedule to open a space for reading the Word?

2. What could you do to enable yourself to read the Scriptures with a more vulnerable heart and mind? What aspects of lectio divina appeal to you most?

3. How have the Scriptures shaped your thoughts, your beliefs, and your actions? How can you continue reading more for transformation than for information?

SPIRITUAL DIRECTION

The Practice of Seeking and Finding God's Guidance

Every Christian should try to consult
some learned person....
Those who walk in the way of prayer
have the greater need of learning;
and the more spiritual they are, the greater their need.

—TERESA OF AVILA, *The Life of Teresa of Jesus*

I began this book by telling you that fifteen years ago a fifteen-minute conversation forever changed my life. During a brief conversation with someone who had been introduced to me as a spiritual director, I unexpectedly encountered Jesus.

Our first few minutes together involved sitting in awkward silence. *This is totally weird and such a waste of my time,* I was thinking. However, toward the end of our visit, with pride checked, I asked with genuine concern, "What would you suggest I *do?*" He responded with, "Who do you believe God created you to *be?*" and I started thinking, *Come on, man. Help me! Don't keep putting it back on me.* I desperately wanted him to take charge, to give me a simple formula for escaping the predicament I found myself in. I came to the retreat feeling more than distraught—I was *desperate* for help.

More dreadful silence followed, and then I offered a reluctant confession that I was fearful, sad, and embarrassed to be a person help-ing others know God while having such a pathetic relationship with God myself. "I honestly don't know what I should do," I whispered. The spiritual director replied softly, "Then perhaps the wise thing would be to do what all desperate people do. Why don't you cry out for help? Tell God what you are really feeling, what you just told me. Don't be afraid. God already knows.... God just wants to hear it from you. Tell him, Fil.... No more games. Just tell God the truth."

This was not the first time I'd been in a desperate situation. Countless times I had cried out to God and been honest in my dis-closure. However, I'd never really come so clean with another person.

For quite some time we sat together. The silence was heavy. The heat of my tears burned my cheeks—the same way those hot tears felt the day when, as a young boy, my brother, Steve, and I had been left home alone. Back then we had such a blast until I knocked a lamp off the table. In these life-illuminating moments, the Holy Spirit of God had begun to reveal the poverty of my soul. The Spirit was exposing the raw and fiercely protected places in my soul that I had not yet offered to the excruciating, healing touch of Jesus. Like the lamp I broke when I was a boy, there was no gluing me back together. Finally, like the bursting of a dam, I told God the truth, all of the truth I knew to tell. For the first time I didn't hold anything back. At the conclu-sion of this makeshift confession, as I was readying to leave, I asked my kind companion about spiritual direction. "Do you think I need a spiritual director?" His smiling response was simply, "How else do you believe you will discover who God created you to be?"

You will discover who God created you to be...what an intrigu-ing idea. I wasn't sure who that person really was. For most of my life I had worked diligently to construct an image reflecting what I felt I must be so that others would love me. I'd always done whatever it took to gain the love of others, so how could I now find the Fil Anderson that God created at the start?

WHAT IN THE WORLD HAPPENED?

Without intending it to happen, I had become a person like Morgan, the middle-aged Baltimore man who takes center stage in Anne Tyler's novel *Morgan's Passing.*

The novel begins with Morgan in a crowd watching a puppet show on a church lawn. Shortly after the show begins, a young man emerges from behind the stage and frantically asks, "Is there a doctor in the house?" After a period of anxious silence, Morgan stands up and says, "I am a doctor." The puppeteer's pregnant wife is in labor. Without seeming to be the least bit alarmed, Morgan escorts the anxious couple to his car and heads to Johns Hopkins Hospital. But before they arrive, the wife shouts, "The baby is here." With no apparent panic, Morgan pulls his car to the curb and delivers the baby. An ambulance arrives and transports the mother and her newborn, along with Morgan and the young father, to the hospital. Once they arrive, as mother and infant are taken into the emergency room, Morgan disappears.

Afterward the couple inquires about Dr. Morgan with the hope of thanking him. No one at the hospital has ever heard of a Dr. Morgan. The new parents are disappointed that they can't express their appreciation.

Four years later Morgan crosses paths with the puppeteer parents. In an uncharacteristic burst of honesty, he admits that he is not really a doctor. In truth, he runs a hardware store. He explains that when they needed help, taking on the role of a doctor was not all that hard. It's an "image thing" he explains: You figure out what people need, and you provide it. Morgan had been doing it his whole life, impersonating therapists, doctors, lawyers, and clergy as the need arose.[1]

I understand Morgan. I had learned to impersonate someone I wanted to be but had never figured out how to be an authentically spiritual person. Only three persons really knew: me, my perceptive and kind friend on the sofa that day at the conference, and of course, God. I appeared to possess a deep awareness of God's presence, but I didn't have a clue where I might find him. I had discovered how to look like a man given to spiritual discipline without ever becoming that man. Like some crafty travel agent, I'd been selling unsuspecting travelers tours to faraway lands that I had never visited. I regularly dispatched folks on spiritual journeys without ever embarking myself. My alienation from God was concealed by my immersion in service for God. What was missing most was a deeply lived love relationship with the One I constantly told others about.

Several weeks ago I was privileged to accompany 150 high school students and their adult friends to Mexico. During the daytime we built homes for six families. During the evening I spoke and invited God to build on our awareness of his character and his love for us.

One of the highlights of the trip was sharing the experience with several men I've known for more than twenty years. When I first met these men, each was in a very different place than where they are today. These very average men who work as professionals in the business sector took a week of vacation to live in tents, cook for teenagers, and help build homes. They have seen "their hearts become seized by the power of a great affection,"[2] and they will never again be the same. When I first met them, they were nominal members of their church, attending on Sundays out of habit or a sense of duty. Their relationship with God was the last thing on their minds. Today they have been taken captive and are being ravished by the love of God.

I experienced a similar transformation. Worse than not telling my high school friends about Jesus when I was a teenager, my adult life had become consumed with telling high school students about Jesus so much that there was no time left for talking with Jesus myself. Like Christopher Columbus, who claimed he had discovered a new world without exploring any more than a shoreline, I had planted my flag on the shore of God's coastline and had never moved beyond the beach.

Yet by God's grace and mercy, I was about to embark on a journey that would carry me into the inner regions of the mystery we know as God. Although I had managed to fool others (I think) and myself (for sure), I now felt hopeful that I could finally live authentically as the man God created me to be. I made a promise to God: "I will not continue living in this way, if you, God, will show me a new way."

A Dramatic Turn

I began thinking that a spiritual director might be just the ticket out of the terrible rushing torrent my life had become. But first I needed to understand spiritual direction and find someone to guide me. My ignorance became a magnificent gift, since it left me with only one Person to ask—Jesus! A world I had known nothing about began opening itself up to me. My cries for help were being answered initially in the form of books on Christian spirituality.[3]

One of these books, *The Genesee Diary: Report from a Trappist Monastery*, consisted of excerpts from the diary of Henri Nouwen, a Catholic priest and university professor who took a sabbatical to live for seven months as a Trappist monk. I related to the disappointment, frustration, and sadness he felt as he considered his busy life. I resonated with his purpose for taking these months away. I gave careful attention to his remarks about visits with his spiritual director. While he had spent years telling others about the importance of solitude, inner freedom, and peace of mind, he admits that he "kept stumbling over his own compulsions and illusions."[4] As he described his painful struggle to understand himself, I found new courage to face the mystery my own life had become. I began to realize that I would know the answers to why my life was running on empty only if I was willing to step back and allow the hard questions to touch me—even if they hurt.

Talking with God about my spiritual malformation, lack of direction, and absence of progress, I felt the terror of going into the dark places of my life. What if I got lost there and never came back? My prayers turned into desperate cries for help: "Do I have to do this alone? Would you please send someone to help me?" Talking with friends and colleagues provided little help. Most of them had never heard of spiritual formation.

Finally, Lucie came in from collecting the day's mail, handed me a newsletter from our church, and pointed to information about an upcoming women's retreat. The guest speaker was a spiritual director who lived in a nearby town. That day I called her and arranged a meeting.

During our first visit over lunch, her attentiveness was striking. Very soon I knew I had met a rare and credible person. She was actually interested in listening to the stories of my life. Occasionally she asked a penetrating question. She was comfortable with periods of silence in our conversation, which were awkward moments for me, moments I desperately worked to fill. More than anything, I felt safe.

As we continued meeting over the course of the next several years, she would answer many questions for me, questions that perhaps I could now answer for others. Questions like: Why do I need a director? Who should be my director? What do I tell my director? One of her most significant gifts was helping me discern my own call to begin offering spiritual direction to others and helping me find a program where I could receive training. However, her most priceless gift was helping me discover how to recognize and listen to the voice of the One who has become the Great Director of my soul.

WHAT IS SPIRITUAL DIRECTION?

A spiritual director is not a superspiritual person who listens to God for you and then tells you what to do. Instead, a spiritual director listens to you and then helps you listen to what God is telling you. A good spiritual director has the gift to be sensitive, present, and supportive to another person in his or her spiritual journey. A spiritual director asks focused questions to help identify the particular path on which God is leading another person. The process is similar to sitting down with a wise friend who is not a trained counselor and pouring out your struggles and confusion. Such a friend will listen carefully, weigh your story, and then if you're fortunate ask a few pointed questions that you know come from a good heart. Those questions are enough to set you on a course that leads you to God's heart. We don't hesitate to seek out professional helpers to assist in curing our diseases, meeting our objectives, or solving our problems. So it seems only natural that one seeking a surer relationship with God would welcome the clarity, guidance, and support that a caring and compassionate spiritual director can provide.

The gifts I have received from spiritual directors include their sensitivity, alertness to my story and my struggles, and their support as I continue my spiritual journey. Spiritual directors have helped me identify the particular path on which God is leading me without telling me the way. None has ever tampered with my freedom to make my own discernments. I have often become confused or disoriented along the way and found it helpful to have a director who could reflect back to me what I was attempting to discern.

Knowing that the spiritual directors who offered their help have traveled the same road I tread is comforting. As I mentioned in an earlier chapter, I spent several weeks traveling in Japan while I was a college student. Days alone in Japan tended to be frightening, unproductive, and sometimes dangerous. However, on the days when my travel guide accompanied me, his familiarity with the language, customs, and terrain made the difference between a rewarding day and an unfulfilled day. In his company I could relax and enjoy my touring. The trip was still my trip; the guide was just there to ensure that I was seeing the most important things along the way and interpreting them correctly.

A Physician's Care

One of my mentors, Tilden Edwards, likens the relationship of a spiritual director to a seeker to that of a physician to a wounded soul.[5] In both kinds of relationships the caregiver provides three essential ingredients: She or he cleans the wound, brings medical attention to the broken parts, and prescribes needed rest. The physician does not heal; rather he or she sets up the environment for the Healer, who is always present and who alone is able to bring healing. The same is true for the spiritual director.

Cleansing the Wound

When I seek spiritual direction, my director recognizes that my first need likely will be for leaving behind or cleansing the accumulation of anxieties, worries, frustrations, disappointments, and fears that crowd my mind. This is a time for letting the fog lift and for becoming aware of God's presence to me and my presence to God. This takes place best in comfortable and quiet surroundings. One of the rules of Saint Benedict concerning spiritual direction states: "Let all guests who arrive be received like Christ, for He is going to say, 'I came as a guest, and you received me.' "[6] My director seems alert to the fact that a simpler, quieter, and aesthetically warmer room will invite a simpler, quieter, and more secure awareness of God's presence. Any ground on which one approaches God is holy and must be treated as such.

Several minutes of silence at the outset of a session are invaluable. A lighted candle has a way of calling our attention to the reality of the Light of the World's presence within and among us. Reading aloud a few sacred words or listening to a softly playing recording of familiar music loosens up the heart, helping us draw our attention to the Holy One. This time is devoted to recollecting ourselves and centering our hearts and minds on being attentive to the One who joins us in the moment.

Brennan Manning describes a busy person who was caught up in the affairs of life and work. He went to a desert hermit to complain about "his frustration in prayer, his flawed virtue, and his failed relationships." The hermit, a man of solitude, listened attentively to his visitor's rehearsal of the struggle and disappointments in leading a Jesus-centered life. He then went into the dark recesses of his cave and came out with a basin and pitcher of water. "Now watch the water as I pour it into the basin," he said. The water splashed on the bottom and against the sides of the container. But the stirred-up water gradually began to settle until finally the small fast ripples gave way to larger swells that oscillated back and forth, and the surface became tranquil and calm, so smooth, in fact, that the visitor could see his face reflected in the placid water.

"That is the way it is when you live constantly in the midst of others. You do not see yourself as you really are because of all the confusion and disturbance. You fail to recognize the divine presence in your life and the consciousness of your belovedness slowly fades."[7]

God is always present, but it takes time for water to settle and become quiet. It's a process that must be waited out; any attempts to hasten it only interfere and stir up the water again. Therefore, at the beginning of a session, my director and I wait for this settling to occur.

Aligning the Broken Parts

After sufficient time for settling and cleansing, the work of alignment begins. This is the time for speaking and listening, for paying attention. I have often wandered into a visit with my spiritual director with no clue about what to discuss. Mostly, I've been so busy and consumed with worry and the troubles of others that I have no idea what God has been saying to me. But as I speak, my spiritual director actively listens, helping me to express my thoughts, feelings, questions, doubts, fears, and experiences in relation to God.

When I come to God, I can bring only the person I really am.

And that person needs all the help I can get. This is particularly true when it comes to paying attention. If I were diagnosed by a specialist, I suspect he would determine that I suffer from GADD—God attention deficit disorder. God's presence and the movement of the Holy Spirit are often so subtle that I miss them completely. Yet they are present in the midst of my life's common events and interactions. Without the assistance of a spiritual companion, I often miss important signs along the way.

Whenever I visit a museum, zoo, or art gallery, I suspect I have broken the time record for making it through from start to finish. It's not that I mind going to those places, it's just that I move about with the end in mind. Lucie, on the other hand, notices things. She takes lots of time, she reads signs, she listens to the comments of the docent, and she closely observes things I would never notice. When we're together in one of these places, it's like having my own personal guide. She slows me down. I imitate her as she pays close attention. I start noticing more, and I walk away feeling like I had fun and learned something too.

Prescribing Rest

Paying attention to God often leads to sightings, signs, or discoveries, and these often lead to choices. When I see God's movement or hear his voice, I am often shown something to do or something to stop doing. The choices are not always easy. Not long ago my spiritual director asked, "How are you going to live with this new awareness? Will you continue living in the house of fear, or will you enter into obedience and enjoy living in the freedom God is calling you toward?"

Spiritual directors have guided me to spiritual disciplines designed to create space in my life for God to be at work. And God alone can conform me to the image of his Son. Without some of these spiritual practices, my awareness of and responsiveness to God's movement would be sorely diminished. I appreciate the challenge of understanding and adding new disciplines, and I value the freedom to relax more and know that my spiritual formation is ultimately God's responsibility, not mine.

Why You Need a Spiritual Director

On more than one occasion I have been confronted with the argument "If I have the Holy Spirit in my life to guide me, why do I need a person to direct me? I can find the way on my own." Let me be clear: The problem does not concern the Holy Spirit. The Holy Spirit leads and guides every one of us, but not every one of us is listening and following. In one of his letters, Saint Bernard boldly expressed his belief in the need for spiritual guides by saying, "He who constitutes himself his own director, becomes the disciple of a fool."[8] My refusal to heed the wise counsel of friends within the community of faith has resulted in some of my greatest embarrassment and sorrow. Often I have been forced to recognize the wisdom of Baron Friedrich von Hügel who said, "Behind every saint stands another saint.... I have never learnt anything myself by my own old nose."[9] I need the counsel of others who know me and who stand with me.

The Scriptures support seeking guidance: "Trust in the LORD with all your heart, and do not rely on your own insight" (Proverbs 3:5). "Plans are established by taking advice; wage war by following wise guidance" (Proverbs 20:18). "Two are better than one, because they have a good reward for their toil. For if they fall, one will lift up the other; but woe to one who is alone and falls and does not have another to help.... And though one might prevail against another, two will withstand one. A threefold cord is not quickly broken" (Ecclesiastes 4:9-10,12).

We all are prone to self-deception. It began when the original man and woman, standing before God, tried to shift blame for their sin. The difference between superficial religiosity and a genuine and sincere spiritual life often is a matter of whether I am allowing my real issues, needs, and problems to present themselves in prayer. My spiritual director helps challenge me to no longer avoid confronting significant personal realities of life.

HOW TO CHOOSE A DIRECTOR

When selecting a spiritual director, look for a person whose desire for spiritual companionship to God is readily apparent. Given the nature of God's character and personal concern for my sound formation, I know that God wants me to benefit from involvement with such a spiritual friend.

If possible, begin with someone you already know. Is there someone to whom you feel a deeper connection and a spiritual resonance? If so, offer him or her to God in prayer. If it would be awkward to be with someone in your circle of acquaintances, I recommend meeting with your pastor to talk about your desire for a spiritual companion. Ask your pastor or others in your faith community for recommendations. Contacting a nearby convent, monastery, or retreat center may also be helpful.

Accompanying my prayer for wisdom in the search for a spiritual director has been the request that God would help me recognize the possibilities that are available. Rather than merely searching for a person who carries the title, I look for someone who possesses the qualities of a spiritual director. The qualities spoken of by Paul to Titus are crucial: "hospitable, a lover of goodness, prudent, upright, devout, and self-controlled…hav[ing] a firm grasp of the word that is trustworthy in accordance with the teaching" (Titus 1:8-9). I need a companion who will help me notice and name my own experience of God so I will recognize the way the Spirit works in my life. At times I need my guide to teach, admonish, or confront me and to hold me accountable for my attitudes and behaviors. However, I have more often needed a companion to encourage and support me, pray for me, listen to me, and share wisdom from his or her own journey.

A simple list may be helpful in focusing your choices. The following guidelines have helped me discern who might be a suitable spiritual director.

Trustworthy and Safe

You want to walk with someone who will not hurt you by betraying your confidences. It's essential that you feel free to tell your spiritual director the complete truth. You need to know that you will not be judged or condemned for your failures.

Humble and Open

You need a guide who is willing to acknowledge that he or she is not perfect but is earnestly seeking the Lord. Look for one who is familiar with human pain and struggle through personal experience, who is open about his or her inadequacies, and who is willing to be vulnerable. You want a guide who sees his or her partially healed wounds as gifts and a sign of God's presence at work in his or her life. Although I don't believe there is a hard-and-fast rule concerning whether your guide be of your gender, it's a matter that should be included in the prayerful discernment of who your director should be.

A Patient and Attentive Listener

You need a guide who is devoted to and open to hearing God and you speak. You want a companion who is able to hear your confessions without being too easily shaken. You need someone who can listen as you bring your strongest, deepest, and darkest feelings into the light with an acknowledgment and understanding of human nature without harsh judgment and criticism.

Balanced Personality

It is important to be with directors who are lighthearted and playful as well as serious-minded and sober. Our resistance to playfulness often rises out of poor self-esteem and a tendency to "spiritualize" everything. Yet we can also use humor to avoid confronting necessary areas of pain and difficulty. You need a director who is alert to these tendencies and who will hold you accountable to a life of integrity and wholeness.

A Wise Questioner

Look for a guide who will ask penetrating questions rather than give you easy answers. An insightful question will often enable you to make a discovery that could lead to a necessary change in your life. You need a director who knows that discernment for your own life lands in your court.

An Outward Focus

A director is a companion on your spiritual journey to come alongside *you*, not to meet a need in his or her life. Most directors are careful to establish and maintain clear boundaries to protect the sanctity of the relationship by not allowing it to become anything other than spiritual direction.

One Matter You Need to Clarify

It's thoughtful and wise to ask your director at your initial meeting whether he or she expects to be paid. Spiritual directors sometimes offer their services on a gratis basis, but not always.

What to Tell Your Director

Initially, several matters need to be discussed and decided. What kind of friendship are you seeking? How often and how long will you meet?

How will sessions be structured? How will the relationship be evaluated and how often? For the relationship to be meaningful, it's crucial that mutual hopes and expectations be clear.

When I began meeting with my first spiritual director (after meeting Brennan Manning), our purpose was to explore who God was in my life. I spoke with her openly about what I actually believed about God. I expressed how God seemed to be working in my life. I explained how God was relating to my marriage, my family, my work, and my relationships with others. I asked about how I could become more alert to God's presence and movement in my life. I sought her wisdom concerning how I might respond to God.

I wanted to get beneath the surface, to become the person God created me to be. I wanted to find a concrete way of living in my relationship with God, a way that would sustain a balance and integration of my intellect and emotions, work and leisure, prayer and play, professional responsibility and personal life. Spiritual direction has put me more in touch with the reality and presence of God, leading to a much more lively and real encounter with God.

THE IMPACT OF SPIRITUAL DIRECTION

Spiritual direction has helped me gain clarity about how I can become the person I really am. Feelings of inadequacy have nipped at my heels for most of my life, but my relationship with spiritual directors has helped me embrace my true identity as a beloved child of God. I've become freer to celebrate my uniqueness, having recognized my distinctive gifts. I've discovered my place in life and have claimed it, I pray, with delight and humility. By an act of God's amazing grace and mercy, experienced profoundly through spiritual direction, I am slowly becoming that kind of person.

I had a most memorable encounter with this kind of freedom after I enrolled in a two-year spiritual guidance program. Part of the training was given during two ten-day residencies. After several days together during our second residency, these thirty people had become my dear and trusted friends. One evening we gathered for a time of guided prayer and meditation. As we were seated in a circle, Tilden Edwards, the director of the program, began to read from 2 Samuel 6, the passage about David's dancing naked before God. (Just then I began to be fearful.) After the reading he explained that in a moment he was going to play some music and, as our prayer, we were going to dance before God. (This is when my fear turned to terror. Getting naked is one thing, but dancing? Well, that's an entirely different matter!) I don't know what kind of childhood trauma led to my dancing phobia. Maybe it was tied to those Weejuns I had to wear to the sock hop that weren't real Weejuns. All I know is that I have few fears greater than dancing in front of others. Even my few attempts to dance when no one was around were deeply troubling experiences.

As the music began, I was frozen with fear. But why? I thought about the people surrounding me. They were kind and caring friends. I looked at the lighted candles and icons. An awareness of God's love for me and my love for God began to come into focus. In a moment my feet began moving. My arms followed. Most amazing, my movement was in rhythm with the music. *I was dancing!* My daughter, an accomplished dancer, would have called it something other than dancing. *Pathetic* comes to mind. My sons would have called it embarrassing, pitiful, or even disgusting. Lucie might have left the room, trying to stifle her laughter. But I was dancing with no concern about how I looked. I was aware only of God and the people who were sharing this experience. I became lost in the wonder and mystery of the moment. An hour later when the music ended, I wept at not being able to dance any longer.

On occasion, as I have reflected back on this experience, I've wondered what God thought of my dancing in prayer. I have concluded that God thought my dancing was original...a one-of-a-kind expression of love. God thought I looked marvelous; *I was being me!*

One of the most beautiful expressions that describes the freedom to be the person God created you to be is found in the apostle Paul's letter to the Christians in Galatia. These are words intended for reading slowly and carefully. Reading them quickly will serve only to diminish their effect.

It is absolutely clear that God has called you to a free life....

My counsel is this: Live freely, animated and motivated by God's Spirit....

What happens when we live God's way? He brings gifts into our lives, much the same way that fruit appears in an orchard—things like affection for others, exuberance about life, serenity. We develop a willingness to stick with things, a sense of compassion in the heart, and a conviction that a basic holiness permeates things and people. We find ourselves involved in loyal commitments, not needing to force our way in life, able to marshal and direct our energies wisely....

Since this is the kind of life we have chosen, the life of the Spirit, let us make sure that we do not just hold it as an idea in our heads or a sentiment in our hearts, but work out its implications in every detail of our lives. That means we will not compare ourselves with each other as if one of us were better and another worse. We have far more interesting things to do with our lives. Each of us is an original. (Galatians 5:13,16,22-23,25-26, MSG)

Running on empty is not how God intended me to live my life. Running on empty is not my identity as a beloved child of God. Precisely because my identity is rooted in God's indescribable, unconditional, unlimited, and eternal love, I can continue on the road to recovery from my addiction to activity and performance and believe with my whole heart that no words describe me better than these: I am a radically beloved child of God.

—POINTS TO PONDER—

1. During the next few days, prayerfully reflect on this question: Am I really awake, aware, and present to God in my life?

2. Seeking clarity in understanding how we should live in relationship with God is difficult to do on our own. If you are not making your spiritual journey with a director, might God be leading you to such a person? Take five or ten minutes to consider the qualities and characteristics of an individual you would look for as a spiritual director.

3. Are you able to imagine yourself talking openly and candidly with someone else about your images of God and your experiences with God?

SORROW

The Weakness That Welcomes
God's Compassion

I think I shall always remember this black period
with a kind of joy, with a pride and a faith
and deep affection that I could not at the time
have believed possible,
for it was during this time
that somehow I survived defeat and lived my life
through to a first completion,
and through the struggle, suffering,
and labor of my own life
came to share some of those qualities
in the lives of people all around me.
—THOMAS WOLFE, *The Autobiography of an American Novelist*

For some reason people seem more comfortable expressing what they think and feel by wearing it on their bumper rather than on their sleeve. One of my favorites: "Men are idiots and I married their king!" Paying attention to the sentiments expressed on bumper stickers may be one of the most overlooked means of knowing what is really going on in people's hearts and minds.

Several years ago the most popular bumper sticker around was "S— Happens!" Although the expression was offensive to some, including those attempting to shield their kids from reading it (especially out loud), it nonetheless reflected the raw truth about everyone's life. I was told of someone who said in an AA meeting, "Truth don't come pretty."

Life can be dastardly difficult. Without so much as a moment's notice, we can be blindsided by struggle, suffering, or sorrow. Faith in God grants crisis immunity to no one. A friend calls and asks if we can get together soon. Sometimes such a call promises good news: a big promotion came through, a baby's on the way, a wayward son or daughter has gotten back on track, or medical tests came back negative. Mostly, however, people call looking for some hope, consolation, or guidance due to the overwhelming burden of life's disappointments and tragedies.

I've experienced countless emotional highs and lows and felt tremendous shifts and changes at the core of my being. There have been days of sorrow and days of happiness. There have been feelings of guilt and feelings of gladness. There have been moments of disappointment and moments of victory. But never has my life been bland or boring. I, too, have been broken, battered, and bruised—yearning desperately for wholeness.

I have been ripped apart by the relentlessly competing demands of my job and home, wife and children, friends and family who persistently ask for more than I've ever felt capable of giving. My hopes for the future have been haunted by the blunders in my past. My desperate longing to get my life right has been dogged by the nagging fear that it will never ever happen, given the obvious fact that I am hopelessly flawed.

So many times I've thought, *If only I were the total package. If only I could repair the broken parts of my life, then everything would be all right.* The words *if only* have always illuminated my disappointment, pain, and anger. For much of my life I've lived in the illusion that whatever condition or circumstance my "if only" focused on, it had the power to right the wrongs and to make me a person everyone else would envy or at least a competent person I could live with—free of the self-judgment that keeps me awake at night. Meanwhile, no one I know, including myself, is living the life we once dreamed of living.

I have lunch with the friend who called. Afterward, as we order a cup of coffee, the conversation becomes more open. "I can't understand why I feel this way," he begins, "but I'm so disappointed with my life. I went to a good college and landed in the perfect job. I married a wonderful lady; we have two great kids and lots of nice things. But my life feels so out of control. I have achieved all I ever thought it would take to make me happy, and yet my life is my biggest disappointment."

YEARNING FOR COMPLETENESS

One of the primary reasons for the hurried and worried, frenzied and frantic pace of my life has been my unceasing yearning for completeness. Longing for a reprieve from the harsh realities of my broken life, I have lived at a relentlessly busy pace, trying to experience completeness or to escape the pain of my untold disappointments. I have lived in the illusion that Jesus had promised me a life without struggle, suffering, and sorrow. He did, in fact pledge: "I came that they may have life, and have it abundantly" (John 10:10). Foolishly, I have lived with the mistaken idea (and a strong preference) that Jesus was offering worldly comforts and pleasures rather than the indescribable gifts of his incomparable friendship. Abundance in life has nothing to do with the absence of suffering.

I shudder when I recall the countless times I have led broken people to believe that if they will entrust their lives to Jesus, their troubles will cease and they will enjoy complete and fulfilling lives. As much curb appeal as this message may have, it's not even close to what God promised. What we see in the Scriptures is actually much greater.

We find the implausible promise that God has broken into our brokenness to find us there, and yet—and this is important—there is no promise anywhere that having found us he will paste our fractured life back together the way we want.

When my children were little, I often returned from out-of-town trips with small gifts. We called them "sursies"—short for "surprises." I still recall the thrill of the children's running into my arms and smothering me with kisses. However, my delight would often fade when they asked the inevitable question, "Daddy, did you bring me a sursie?" This question always had a way of exposing their sincere interests. They wanted me, but they were quick to look for the latest sursie!

To my dismay I find that my interest in God often has more to do with the disappointing condition of my circumstances than my longing for intimacy with God. I'd rather have his healing and restoration than his friendship. I've spent most of my life hoping and praying that God would make me complete and, for Pete's sake, just take away this suffering and sorrow! But I've found myself living between groundless hope, frustration, and disappointment, knowing the whole time that I am still incomplete. Try as I might to find guarantees of completeness in the Scriptures, they simply aren't there. There is one gift that God promises, and that gift is God. This gift is the only reality in the universe that completes us.

A PLAUSIBLE THREAT

One of my greatest concerns for the church as it responds to an increasingly complex and challenging culture is its death grip on sentimentality. The American church's view of life often poses a real threat to its credibility. I find myself agreeing with the criticism I hear from those who lay no claim to friendship with God as they express their disgust over most churches' schmaltzy, pie-in-the-sky view of life. You know the implausible stories as well as I do: Someone has lived a difficult life, beaten down by some handicap or hardship, until God enters the picture and rescues him (or her) from painful circumstances. No longer is life a disappointing struggle. With God on the person's side, he or she becomes complete and "more than a conqueror," clinging to promises interpreted to the person's own liking. Then come the handpicked verses: "We know that all things work together for good for those who love God, who are called according to his purpose" (Romans 8:28). The result of such teaching is a mass of gullible, misguided people inviting others to join in the illusion while overlooking a multitude of other biblical passages, the message of which any right-thinking person would prefer to ignore.

Archbishop William Temple, a writer, theologian, and philosopher in the first half of the twentieth century, observed that Christians are fond of trying to be more spiritual than God. When Jesus encountered difficulty or found himself in pain, after great struggle he embraced the pain and allowed it to happen. He discovered what it feels like to experience a sense of God's absence. When he cried out, while on the cross, "My God, where are you? Why have you forsaken me?" Jesus wasn't merely reciting the psalmist's experience, he was telling us his own.[1] Had we heard Jesus continue, he might have said, "I have cried urgently for help, but you have ignored me." If Jesus meant what he said about God's seeming abandonment, he was blaming God in the moment of his vulnerability.

Just before Jesus set out on his journey from the Upper Room to Gethsemane and finally to Calvary, he spoke openly with his closest followers about how their relationship with him would drastically change when he departed for heaven. He spoke candidly about the things they should expect. Finally he said, "I've told you all this so that trusting me, you will be unshakable and assured, deeply at peace. In this godless world *you will continue to experience difficulties.* But take heart! I've conquered the world" (John 16:33, MSG).

I have discovered that knowing what to expect brings a certain peace. Perhaps this is what Jesus had in mind when he said, "The truth will set you free."[2] The truth we have from Jesus is simple and clear: As long as we're living in this world, we will have difficulties. Sometimes we create our own difficulties, and at other times they find us. But we can rest assured that we will run into trouble. And on certain days, as Jesus promised, our lives will dissolve into chaos.

Since leaving a long career in youth ministry several years ago, I interviewed for two positions. I was confident of God's leading in the process, and I was certain that I'd be the candidate selected. Both times I was denied my dream job. Both times I was devastated beyond words, my confidence was shaken, and my future was left frighteningly uncertain.

During one of those dreadfully dark times, I recalled the lesson learned by Viktor Frankl from his horrific experience in the Nazi death camps. He described the times when there is nothing we can do to change our circumstances as a time when we are nonetheless free to decide our response to the pain and injustice. As Frankl declared, "Everything can be taken away from man except for one final thing—the last of human freedoms—to choose one's attitude in any given set of circumstances, to choose one's own way.... [Despite the conditions in the death camps], in the final analysis it becomes clear that the sort of person the prisoner became was the result of inner decision, and not the result of camp conditions alone."[3] As I reflect on my life today, it's apparent I have gained far more than I've lost during this trying season. In the middle of all that was painful, I encountered God.

FINDING JOY THROUGH TEARS

As I listen carefully to the saints who lived before and those living now, I find no reason to question the value of suffering and sorrow.

Listening to the hard-won wisdom gained through their endurance, I begin to wonder if in my avoidance of these things I have been missing out on the very thing my heart has yearned for most: intimacy with God. One of those saints who experienced both pain and God's intimacy wrote, "God whispers to us in our pleasures, speaks in our conscience, but shouts in our pains; it is his megaphone to rouse a deaf world."[4]

Could it be true that the highest joy often comes in the deepest sorrow? In the corner of the world where I live, a radical distinction has been made between joy and sorrow. Life has taught me to believe that when I'm glad, I can't be sad, and when I'm sad, I can't be glad. For this reason I do everything I can to keep sadness and gladness separated. Sadness and distress have to be kept away, because they are the opposites of the happiness and contentment for which I long. Difficulty in all its forms must be held at bay for the simple reason it will prevent me from experiencing the completeness for which I strive. Difficulties are obstructions on the way to happiness—which is the goal of life—or so I thought.

The life-view offered by Jesus stands in sharp contrast to the world's view and to that of many churches. Jesus shows in his teachings and in his life that true joy often is hidden in the midst of sadness, that the abundant life he offers often finds its beginnings in difficulty. He says, "Unless a grain of wheat falls into the earth and dies, it remains just a single grain; but if it dies, it bears much fruit. Those who love their life lose it, and those who hate their life in this world will keep it.... Whoever serves me must follow me" (John 12:24-26). The words of A. W. Tozer reassure us: "The Bible was written in tears and to tears it yields its best treasures."[5] The closest communion with God, I have begun to discover, comes through the shedding of my tears. If grapes and grain are not crushed, there can be no wine and bread. If my life is not crushed, there will not be the closest and most intimate communion with God.

I can recall a time when I hoped to never cry again, but more recently I have hoped to cry more often. Frederick Buechner was right. Tears tell me something about the secret of who I really am. My tears lead me to my heart, where I have encountered God and discovered what God treasures most. This represents a whole new way of living, a way in which pain can be embraced, not out of some neurotic desire to suffer, but in the awareness that something new will be born. Jesus says: "When a woman is in labor, she has pain, because her hour has come. But when her child is born, she no longer remembers the anguish because of the joy of having brought a human being into the world" (John 16:21).

MODERN-DAY HEROES

A friend and I were watching an NBA game, and afterward we couldn't help noticing a large group of people, young and old, clamoring for the autographs of several players. Among these modern-day heroes were men with physical strength, athletic ability, and large salaries, but they nonetheless fell far below my standard for heroes.

For the next several days I pondered the question, "Who are my heroes and what are my criteria?" My heroes are inconsistent, weak-kneed, and wobbly, inclined to believe their lives are a disappointment to God. My heroes are those whose faith has not protected them from facing crises, but their faith has brought from the crises a most remarkable gift: grace—the unexpected, unexplainable, undeserved gift of God's love. My heroes are women and men who know that any god who guarantees protection from struggle, suffering, and sorrow while assuring the fulfillment of all their desires is a quack whose treatments only worsen the disease. My heroes know they have a God who loves them so intensely that there is no painful or shameful experience where God will not willingly meet them.

Dale: Gratitude in an Early Death

In 1999 I sat in my office with the brother-in-law of one of my closest friends. At the time, Dale, a forty-year-old husband, father, and beloved son of God, was fighting a courageous battle against cancer. As he reflected on life, as if reciting a Thanksgiving Day litany, he named the things he was most grateful for.

"I've had an awesome life," he told me. "I was loved in a special way while growing up. I was fortunate to go to college, and I've been able to own a business and provide service for people I enjoy. I have the most wonderful wife and two of the best sons a father could ever wish for. And I've known the love of God. How my life seems to be ending is not what I had in mind, but in the process I've been learning that life is really all about not knowing, having to make adjustments, taking each moment as it comes and making the best of it, without really knowing what's going to happen next."

When he left my office, I prayed that I would always remember the intensity of his words. I think often of his statement: "If I were to die tomorrow, there is nothing in me that would wish to believe I have been cheated. God has given me a great life, one that I prefer to measure by its depth and quality rather than its duration." Then he added, "I've had my share of difficulties and challenges, and it appears the last may be to die in a manner that never causes my sons to wonder whether God is kind and good."

A month later Dale died a hero.

Steve: Lighthearted in Suffering

During the twenty-five years that I served on the staff of a Christian ministry, I was surrounded daily by extraordinarily talented people. Instead of a welcome blessing, however, it was one of the most difficult challenges I confronted. I spent most days feeling intimidated, fearful, and overwhelmed by a sense of my inferiority. As a result, I didn't wish that I could be more like these other leaders…I actually wished I could *be* them.

One of these talented colleagues was one of the most effective communicators I've ever known. He possessed sage wisdom, was profoundly insightful, and exhibited an enviable light and tender heart. People were naturally attracted to this man, so I wanted to be him. Then I learned of his life's difficulties and suffering.

One of the first things I learned about Steve was of his mentally retarded brother and the challenges he faced growing up with a brother who was different. Then I discovered that while Steve was in high school, another beloved brother was killed in an automobile accident. Not long after he married, his mother died. Then two of his sons were diagnosed with Tourette's syndrome, a neurobiological condition characterized by multiple motor and vocal tics. While Steve's father was in the latter stages of Lou Gehrig's disease, his sister fought a valiant battle with cancer and died. Months later his father died.

I can't help but believe it was in the furnace of these afflictions that the qualities I most envied were forged. God appears to equip people for service while they struggle through places of sorrow and suffering. I believe that's where God found my friend Steve.

Geran: Finding Hope in Devastating Loss

For three summers our daughter, Meredith, returned home from college to work as a baby-sitter for a family with three young boys. The experience was life-transforming, as *her boys* shared the daily suffering of their dad, Geran. Beginning in 1997 Geran was dying slowly from the effects of Lou Gehrig's disease.

When asked, "How in the world can a dying man be happy?" the short answer Geran gave was, "I'm not dead yet!" But there was more to it. While he had lost all of his physical abilities, he had not lost his faith in God, the love of his family, his joy in living, and his sense of humor.

Geran was steadfast in believing that God was completely in control. As he said, "God has made it clear that we are to trust him completely, yet that doesn't mean that I haven't shed tears. It's a terribly sad thing." Geran took to heart the apostle Paul's words "neither death, nor life, nor angels, nor rulers, nor things present, nor things to come...will be able to separate us from the love of God" (Romans 8:38-39). For him this was no theory but a matter of indisputable truth.

Before the publication of this book, Geran reached the end of his earthly journey. At his memorial service I was given a copy of an essay he had written on the fifth anniversary of his diagnosis. He described the meeting with his doctor with heart-wrenching sadness: "While driving home I was overcome with the deepest sense of anguish that I've ever experienced." He began to cry as he had never cried before: "In that moment of deep anguish I cried out to God, 'Why?'" Within moments God responded: "Remember this, had any other condition been better for you than the one in which you [find yourself], divine love would have put you there."

Then Geran, this modern-day hero, declared, "By the grace of God the answer to the question 'Why?' was apparent...and I haven't been compelled to ask it again. What was not immediately apparent was how God would give me the strength to persevere as my disease progressed."

Until the very end, Geran was resolute in his belief that, because God is in control, his illness could not be an accident, mistake, or oversight. An avid backpacker, often he likened his illness to a hiking trip. Admitting it was "the toughest one yet," his confidence never wavered that "the view from the top will be glorious and will make it all worthwhile."

Tripp: Standing Strong in Affliction

For several years a magnet on the door of our refrigerator has held a card bearing the words of Psalm 121. The words offer assurance of

God's careful and loving protection. A close friend named Tripp sent the card to us during a terribly stormy season in his life. Even on his darkest days, he demonstrated remarkable courage and concern for how his affliction might be impacting the lives of those he loves.

When Tripp was a freshman in high school, we became friends; by the time he was a senior, we had become soul mates. When he was in college, together we faced his uncertain future as the presence of a temporal-lobe brain tumor the size of an egg was discovered. Since that time I have watched Tripp suffer physically, but perhaps even more, emotionally. However, more than anyone I know, Tripp has brought meaning to Brother André's words, "If we truly knew the value of suffering, we would ask the good God for it."[6] God has graced Tripp with the ability to believe that afflictions are not a sign of God's absence but rather his presence.

Today, Tripp and his wife, Anna, serve on the staff of InterVarsity Christian Fellowship at the University of Tennessee. Due to his medical history, Tennessee law prohibits him from driving. Rather than facing this news as a setback, he quickly realized that the only way to get to campus, the grocery store, or anywhere else was to take the city bus. After riding the bus several times, he learned that his inability to drive was in fact an amazing gift, providing him with the opportunity to continually meet wonderful people.

There are, he admits, times when he is sad for Anna, who has to run all of their errands and take him places that are not on the bus line. He also admits it can be frustrating when it takes him hours to do things it might otherwise take only a few minutes to accomplish.

"Some would say, 'Yikes! What a pain!'" he said. "I disagree! Today was a great day. I have become friends with Penny (an anthropologist who tells me pastor jokes and loves to see me smile), Bried (a kind Irish woman who loves shade in the summertime), Herbert (a God-fearing black gentleman born in 1907 who used to ride his horse to work), Shawna (a young woman with satanic tattoos), Ron (a retired man who is 'not on a schedule and full of time'), Brian (a geologist with a long goatee and a lot of wisdom), Charles (a man who loves to play the trombone with his eighth-grade son), Jeremiah (a skinny, Spirit-filled black man who was in a wheelchair for four years until the Lord told him to walk), Brady Wilson (a fragile old man who always has his harmonica), Richard (who was once a mason and now drives the bus and sings Southern gospel music with the group Heartfelt), and the other bus drivers (Skip, Julie, Jeff, Paulette, and Debby) who are full of excitement. I have found great joy in loving them and speaking to them about my Lord Jesus Christ. I wouldn't change a thing!"

Whenever Tripp and I visit, I grow stronger in my belief that his struggles have provided him a clearer and more vibrant view of God.

Grimes: Healing amid Grief

As I mentioned before, Lucie, our children, and I have been enriched by having others live in our home. One of our houseguests was a college student named Grimes. While he was in high school, his father died. While he was in college, his mother died. Late one summer evening while we sat together on the back porch, he described his struggles: "While I was supposed to be experiencing the best years of my life, without any warning I woke up and discovered I was a homeless orphan."

The gift I was given by my "son" Grimes was that of letting me see and even enter with him into his pain. Grimes never ran from it. Rather, he embraced his pain and demonstrated relentless courage as he lived in the belief that beyond his very real pain was a place of healing that he was slowly moving toward. He wept and grieved over his losses so that, without any attachment to or melancholy about the past, he could finally become free to live wholly in the new place God was leading him to.

Emily Dickinson, in her poem "A Great Hope Fell," refers to the death of an undisclosed longing and her effort to deny the overwhelming loss. She recognized that refusing to acknowledge her pain had precariously enlarged it:

> Until it grew so wide
> That all my Life had entered it.[7]

While Grimes was living in our home, he faced the frightening prospect that is always inherent in pain: that it will remain forever—leading to nothing but greater pain. However, with raw and rare courage, this young man resisted the urge to remain stuck in his pain and the consequence that surely would have followed. Rather than allow the pain to create a dead end, he acknowledged and expressed his pain, and in so doing, Grimes gained a profoundly clear view of God and opened the way for God to enter more intimately into his life.

No Magic Answers

Some time ago I received a letter from a close friend who had been weathering one of life's storms. I read his letter intently as he reflected on the dramatic changes that his struggle had produced. Then he offered these insights: "I am learning that for life's troubles there are often no magic answers, no silver bullet. All I can do is live each moment as it comes and be aware of God in it. This is my life right now…the daily challenge to be awake. I want to let struggle, grief, and hurt exist side by side with joy, peace, and hope." Perhaps the portion of his letter I appreciated most was its conclusion. He signed it: "Wounded but still walking." I couldn't help but think, *Aren't we all?*

Some days I wonder, especially after reading a letter like his, where I got the idea that God promises us a life of fulfillment and completeness that's devoid of suffering. Any thoughtful reading of the Scriptures forces me to acknowledge that not all the stories have happy endings. Not all of my heroes in the Scriptures laid hold of the promises they pursued. "The only land we are certain Abraham owned at the end of his life was the burial plot he purchased for Sarah. Moses only got close enough to the promised land to see it from the mountain where he died. David's life certainly didn't end on a high note."[8] And because I am often so self-consumed, I have a tendency to believe God's history is restricted to my span of life and his promises are going to be delivered just before the buzzer sounds. Reading the Scriptures, biographies of Christians, and the sacred writings of many across the span of history has helped me live with a broader view of human history and God's involvement in it.

The psalms are glaringly honest in their expression of this truth:

My God, my God, why have you forsaken me?
  Why are you so far from helping me, from the words of
    my groaning?
O my God, I cry by day, but you do not answer;
  and by night, but find no rest.

Yet you are holy,
  enthroned on the praises of Israel. (Psalm 22:1-3)

The amazing and sometimes baffling thing about David, the author of this and many other psalms, was his uncanny ability to trust in the ultimate goodness and trustworthiness of God while at the same time suffering from God's seeming absence. David possessed a ruthless confidence in God. I, on the other hand, have been conditioned to flinch at even small struggles and fleeting sorrows. I am inclined to deny the harsh inevitability of pain, numbing my mind and heart through distractions, pretending things will certainly be better soon.

STORMY SAILING

One of my favorite stories of the life of Jesus is recorded in the fourth chapter of Mark's gospel. Jesus has spent a day with crowds of broken people. At day's end he announces to his friends that it's time to head to the other side of the Sea of Galilee. As they sail into the night, a storm blows up, and the boat begins taking on water. To the seasoned sailors on board, the magnitude of the problem is apparent. Meanwhile, to their great chagrin, they discover Jesus sound asleep. They awake him with the obvious question: "Do you not care that we are perishing?" (Mark 4:38). After Jesus commands the sea, "Quiet! Settle down!" the wind runs out of breath. Jesus reprimands the disciples (remember, these were men he loved more than his own life): "Why are you such cowards? Don't you have any faith at all?" (Mark 4:39-40, MSG). I can easily imagine Jesus continuing, "Haven't you guys gotten it yet? Don't you understand I have the power either to calm the storm or to calm you while the storm rages?"

This story illustrates a huge fact of life that I have needed to relearn: There is no immunity from life's storms, even when I'm living in the intimacy of a close friendship with God. In fact, I am inclined to believe that a relationship with God *improves* the odds that I might wind up in even more storms. The journey through life with God provides countless ups and downs and twists and turns, but if I hang in there I will find that God never changes. I was ushered into life out of God's love. I am sustained in life by God's love. I am called to return to God's love. Through life's difficult and disappointing experiences, I am held tenderly in God's strong hand.

Just as the best time to take a vacation is before you feel a desperate need for one, the best time to prepare for life's inevitable suffering is before you begin to suffer. Plunging more deeply into the cavernous wonder and mystery of God's relentless love, as spiritual direction has led me to do, has been wonderful preparation for more fully living and embracing pain and suffering when they appear.

God and Dark Clouds

I'll never forget the Saturday a few years ago when I drove to the funeral of some very dear friends. Taylor and Mary Ann Odom—friends I had known for two decades—and four of their six children had been killed in a car accident. The reading for the day of the service, in Oswald Chambers's *My Utmost for His Highest*, spoke profoundly to the painful mystery of God's providence demonstrated in the death of these six people. The memory of Chambers's insights provided me remarkable solace as I viewed the six white caskets lining the front of the sanctuary.

Chambers explains that in the Bible there is always a connection made between clouds and God. Clouds are used to symbolize sorrow or suffering within or without our personal lives, which seem to dispute the rule of God. Chambers expresses how life's sorrows and sufferings have a way of teaching us to live by faith. He goes so far as to say that if there were not these struggles then we would have no faith.

> "The clouds are the dust of His feet" (Nahum 1:3). They are a sign that God is there. What a revelation to know that sorrow, bereavement, and suffering are actually the clouds that come along with God! God cannot come near us without clouds—He does not come in clear-shining brightness.
>
> It is not true to say that God wants to teach us something in our trials. Through every cloud He brings our way, He wants us to unlearn something. His purpose in using the cloud is to simplify our beliefs until our relationship with Him is exactly like that of a child....
>
> Until we can come face to face with the deepest, darkest

fact of life without it damaging our view of God's character, we do not yet know Him.[9]

The apostle Paul learned to live with his eyes focused on Jesus, the "author and perfecter" of his faith. Paul was a man who could look at dim reality and see the bright face of God. Yet living in intimate communion with God did not land him a place on Easy Street. Here's just a sampling of what his life was like:

> Five times I have received from the Jews the forty lashes minus
> one. Three times I was beaten with rods. Once I received a
> stoning. Three times I was shipwrecked; for a night and a day
> I was adrift at sea; on frequent journeys, in danger from rivers,
> danger from bandits, danger from my own people, danger
> from Gentiles, danger in the city, danger in the wilderness,
> danger at sea, danger from false brothers and sisters; in toil
> and hardship, through many a sleepless night, hungry and
> thirsty, often without food, cold and naked. And, besides other
> things [what in the world could he have left out?], I am under
> daily pressure because of my anxiety for all the churches.
> (2 Corinthians 11:24-28)

As I read Paul's litany of suffering and sorrow I can't help but imagine the toll these difficulties would have taken on me. What he describes goes way beyond my threshold of pain. I have seen the cheese slide off my cracker before, and it didn't take nearly as much torment as Paul endured. Nonetheless, Paul continues his story with these remarkable words:

> We've been surrounded and battered by troubles, but we're not
> demoralized; we're not sure what to do, but we know that God

knows what to do; we've been spiritually terrorized, but God hasn't left our side; we've been thrown down, but we haven't broken....

So we're not giving up. How could we! Even though on the outside it often looks like things are falling apart on us, on the inside, where God is making new life, not a day goes by without his unfolding grace. These hard times are small potatoes compared to the coming good times, the lavish celebration prepared for us. There's far more here than meets the eye. The things we see now are here today, gone tomorrow. But the things we can't see now will last forever. (2 Corinthians 4:8-9,16-18, MSG)

LIFE LESSONS

Years ago my son Will came home after having crashed his bike. A quick look at his badly injured chin was all it took for us to load him into the car and rush him to nearby Wesley Long Hospital. Our family doctor arrived and with great care began to give the nurses and me our assignments. My task was to stand at Will's feet and look into his pain-filled eyes. Our doctor said, "Will, whatever you do, don't turn your eyes away from your dad's eyes."

Will's frightened, pain-filled eyes peered deeply into mine. I sensed that he was looking for something in my eyes that he desperately needed. Was it assurance that he was going to be okay, that he would be able to endure the pain, or that he was not going to be left alone?

As our eyes locked on to one another's, a nurse produced a syringe containing Novocain, with a needle about six inches long and the thickness of pencil lead. After injecting the painkiller into the jaw just above my son's chin, another nurse and a doctor began cleaning the wound with Betadine, pulling small pieces of dirt and gravel from the wound. Then the sewing began. I believe it was looking into each other's eyes that got us both through that difficult experience.

Not long ago I listened to a dear friend who has a great sense of humor as he talked about his life and all its struggle, suffering, and sorrow. Then he stopped and said, "Look, I know I'm not much, but I'm all that I ever think about."

———————

I know what my friend means. I too can easily become preoccupied, consumed, and then overwhelmed with my life's struggles. But I can choose to shift my focus and occupy my soul with looking not at my present trials (without ignoring or denying them) but into the face of Jesus. When I make this a regular and passionate occupation, my soul becomes more tranquil and still, and therefore more able to reflect the God it adores. When this occurs, the busyness diminishes and the pace of my life becomes more sane and humane. When I look into the face of Jesus, I discover what my heart has yearned for, far more than fulfillment and pleasure. "As a deer longs for flowing streams, so my soul longs for you, O God. My soul thirsts for God, for the living God" (Psalm 42:1-2).

—POINTS TO PONDER—

1. When you feel sad, lonely, vulnerable, or hurt, how do you find God *within* these experiences? How have you felt his loving touch in times of pain?

2. How can you make sorrow an ally in your daily journey with God?

3. Has sorrow enhanced your intimacy with God, or has it threatened your intimacy?

10

JOY

God's Echo in Our Lives

Life need not be easy to be joyful.
Joy is not the absence of trouble
but the presence of Christ.

—WILLIAM VANDER HOVEN

The single word that sums up my life fifteen years ago is *absurd*. I didn't realize it, though, until I discovered the origin of the word. *Absurd* has its roots in the Latin *ab*, meaning "away from" or "completely," plus *surdus*, meaning "deaf, dull, or unwilling to hear; insensible." To live an absurd life is to live away from listening or completely without hearing. What made my life absurd was my unwillingness to hear the voice of God speaking to me—most critically about my identity.

I had missed the correct answer to a crucial question: Who am I? Although I don't recall posing this question in so many words, I was seeking the answer in my day-to-day decisions and actions. Assuming the wrong answers to be authoritative, I became misshapen in my identity and misguided in where I thought I was going. Sadly, I was deaf to the voice of God, the only source of the true answer to the "Who am I?" question. Instead, the answers I listened for were those of my own making: "I am what I do. I am what others say about me. I am what I have. I am what I feel." My reputation, accomplishments, possessions, and emotions defined who I was.

When my self-definition is based on my success, popularity, power, or feelings, my identity is an illusion. Clearly and profoundly, Jesus persists, whether or not I'm listening: "Fil, you are not what the world says or thinks about you; you are my little brother, the son of my Father, and I love you, and that alone is your true identity." His loving persistence overwhelms me.

Each day it's absolutely crucial for me to listen for God's voice, affirming that I am God's beloved child. Only then can I resist the temptation to reinhabit my false identity. Only when I am listening to God's voice, and not my own, am I set free from having to prove to the world (or to myself) that I am worth loving, because God has already, repeatedly, affirmed his love for me.

GOD'S GIFT OF JOY

Knowing that I am the apple of God's eye has re-formed my life in love, by bringing incredible joy into my life. Jesus made known to me his Father's love so that his joy could become mine and so that my joy could be absolute. Joy is what happens when I know I am loved unconditionally and that nothing I gain or lose can take away that love or the joy that follows it.

As I write these words, their meaning and impact stun me. My most sensible response is to stand amazed: "This is incredible! The God of the universe, the One who created me, is outrageously in love with me." How could I not be full of joy when I remember, "The LORD, your God, is in your midst, a warrior who gives victory; he will rejoice over you with gladness, he will renew you in his love; he will exult over you with loud singing" (Zephaniah 3:17).

Author John Ortberg has led me to conclude that the most vivid sign of a follower of Jesus is not faith, hope, or even love, but joy. "Joy is at the heart of God's plan for human beings. The reason for this is worth pondering awhile: Joy is at the heart of God himself. We will never understand the significance of joy in human life until we understand its importance to God."[1] Fortunately, the more I understand the importance God places on living joyfully, the more I understand the significance of joyful living.

G. K. Chesterton is another author who understood the centrality of joy in the nature and character of God. His writings reflect a childlike quality to the ways God approaches all created things that speak of the joy in his heart. Picture a playground full of happy children running wildly and laughing uncontrollably without a care in the world. The joy seen in the most delighted child is but an inkling of the joy that lies within the heart of God. I want to stand up and shout (and maybe even dance) when I hear Chesterton speak of God as having "the eternal appetite of infancy" while, on the other hand, we "have sinned and grown old, and our Father is younger than we."[2] That's why the image of the little Down syndrome boy on the beach stays with me. There, running full speed toward me, his arms flung wide open, I stood eye to eye with the eternal appetite of infancy, and his lips smothered my face with kisses. That's joy!

Whatever else we need to comprehend about God, I'm convinced we will not understand him until we know this: God is the most joyful Being in the universe. And yet this most joyful God knows sorrow and sadness. Jesus is affectionately referred to as "a man of sorrows, and acquainted with grief" (Isaiah 53:3, NASB). But thanks be to God, the sorrow of God is only a temporary response to our broken and bewildered world. Sorrow and sadness do not reflect the essential character of God. Joy is God's perpetual and eternal disposition.

It follows then that God wants all that he created to reflect the joy that is central to his character. God undoubtedly inspired Henry van Dyke to pen the words, "Joyful, joyful we adore Thee.... Hearts unfold like flowers before Thee."[3] How could we adore God if we did not know his character, and how could we know his character and not be joyful? All of God's creation, and especially we who are made in his image, are designed to reflect God's relentless joy in life.

Scripture speaks often of joy, and it is required of God's followers at all times. Paul wrote, "Celebrate God all day, every day. I mean, *revel* in him!" (Philippians 4:4, MSG). C. S. Lewis reminds us that "Joy is the serious business of heaven."[4] When you think about it, living without joy is a serious offense against God. Yet, as it's been sadly noted, joylessness "may be the sin most readily tolerated by the church."[5] If we really believed the things we say about God's power and control, we'd lighten up. We'd be more playful. Some of us would become playful perhaps for the first time since childhood. Would God be upset if Christians became known for fun, laughter, and joy? "The problem with people, according to Jesus, is not that we are too happy for God's taste, but that we are not happy enough."[6] Instead of Christians moping around and wringing our hands at the condition of the world, perhaps we should strike up a game of Birdie on the Perch or Red Rover.

GOD LIVES IN JOY

One morning a Sunday school teacher asked her young students the question all kids are asked: "Where does God live?" Immediately one of the boys replied, "I know! I know! God lives in our bathroom." Puzzled by his answer, the teacher asked, "Why do you believe that?" He responded, "Because every morning my dad bangs on the door and says, 'My God, are you still in there?'" Although you may be more concerned with this dad's use of God's name, I'd like to redirect your attention to the young boy's provocative discernment.

This story conveys a profound truth about the marvel and mystery of God. (And oftentimes we need a child to point these things out.) If I believe the Bible, I must believe that God lives everywhere…even in my bathroom. I must also learn to live in light of God always being present in all places and in view of his outrageous love for me. The awareness of his presence and his love will color and shape my life to its core. This awareness will usher me into a place of joy that those around me may find either admirable or foolish. But why should I worry about that?

While I was writing this book, I started developing a case of "terminal seriousness." Somehow the hours of introspection and laboring over finding just the right words began to take their toll. One Sunday as I walked into church, a friend handed me a letter. He had recently attended a retreat I directed. In the moments before worship began, I opened the letter. The initial lines were kind and affirming. Then he added, "Fil, I see you as a man deeply moved with tears of sadness and concern for others.… However, I feel the Lord wants you to experience the same level of connection with Him through wild outbursts of laughter and joy.… I believe God wants you to risk your vanity by laughing from the gut more often.… David may have looked like a fool when he danced, but God was honored. I hope you spend the rest of your life joyfully praising God like a fool." My friend's hope for me has become my own hope. I yearn to be more attentive to my level of joy and make the choice to be joyful more often.

The Fifth Gospel is a two-hour solo drama that Craig McNair performed for over twenty years. Author Mike Yaconelli describes one of its classic scenes in which Jesus and the disciples are all in the river taking baths when the beloved disciple, John, reaches down to the river's floor and brings up a huge mud pie. "Preoccupied with their washing, none of the disciples notices. John takes careful aim at his favorite target, Peter. SPLAT! The mud pie strikes Peter in the face. John immediately ducks underwater as though he is scrubbing. Peter reaches for his own mud pie, takes careful aim at Matthew, and lets it fly. WHAM! James wastes no time responding with his own mud pie, and soon bedlam breaks out amongst the disciples. A full-fledged mud fight is under way."[7] *(Are you beginning to want to join in on their fun?)* "Philip and Bartholomew sneak up on Judas, whom they didn't particularly like anyway, and nail him with two mud pies. Simon the Zealot, who has never been particularly close to John because he thinks he's a wimp, lets loose with a huge mud pie. John ducks and the mud missile hits Jesus right in the middle of his forehead. All the disciples freeze. After a long silence Thomas leans over to Simon and says, 'You idiot! You just hit the Son of God with a mud pie.... He'll turn us into turtles!' Jesus gazes slowly at each of the disciples, each one fearing the worst. With a knowing smile, Jesus stops when he sees Simon, who refuses to look in Jesus' eyes. Jesus reaches down into the mud and comes up with a very large mud pie and—and BAM!— Simon is hit squarely on the top of his head, and as the mud slithers down his face, everyone, including Jesus, breaks into laughter."[8]

Is this a difficult scenario for you to imagine? I hope it isn't. I believe Jesus was as playful as he was prayerful. I believe it grieves his heart to see how gloomy followers of his have caused people searching for real life to stay away from its source. James Joyce wrote in his novel *A Portrait of the Artist As a Young Man* of his hero's reason for choosing not to become a priest. Stephen Dedalus had a frightening vision of what would likely happen to his face, how it would become like that of other religious people he knew, "a mirthless mask reflecting a sunken day...sour-faced and devout, shot with pink tinges of suffocated anger."[9] In particular, so many of the high school folks I have known, who held no interest in God, were attracted to him when they finally encountered his joy in the lives of others.

I'll never forget a phone call I received years ago on a Saturday morning.

"Fil, this is Eric's mom. Can you tell me what happened to him? He's not the same person!"

"I'm not certain I know what you're referring to," I replied.

"Ever since he came home from that camp, Eric's been a different person. He's so happy and pleasant to be around. Whatever happened, his dad and I want to thank you."

Eric was a typical high school junior. Most weekends he went out with his buddies, carousing. His grades were not a priority, his future was not something that concerned him, and he was a pain for his parents to endure. He was headed for a certain fall when he went to camp with a bunch of his friends and me the summer before his senior year.

During that week of camp Eric discovered that Jesus is hopelessly in love with him. He was shocked to find that nothing he could ever do would make Jesus love him more. And nothing he ever did would make Jesus love him less. Eric returned home having realized for the first time that the love of Jesus is the most prevailing and magnificent force in the world. It's stronger than every rejection, every failure, every tragedy, every worry, and every hurt.

Indeed, there is a being in the world who wants us to live joylessly, in sadness, but it is certainly not God. The great teacher and confessor Frances de Sales said, "The evil one is pleased with sadness and melancholy because he himself is sad and melancholy, and will be so for all eternity. Hence he desires that everyone should be like himself."[10]

Joy is the most perfect and reliable evidence we will ever have of the presence of God. This is why protecting joy is so important. It would be just like the Evil One to try to steal it, since joy is our most vital sign of connection with God. Terrible things happen: chaos, broken hearts, failure, anxiety, and sometimes awful news interrupting our sleep in the middle of the night. Trouble is to be expected in this life, but misery, well, that's optional.

RESTORING OUR JOY

It is sometimes hard work, not letting darkness overtake us, robbing us of our joy. Thankfully, we have the psalms to guide us back to God's heart of joy. A careful reading of the psalms offers the framework for all elements of the soul. In them, no emotion is disallowed. In the safe company of our merciful God, we are free to express any feeling— even when we feel betrayed or abandoned by God.

When I offer to God the words of the Spirit-guided prayers from the psalms, my concerns lead me to God. In the middle of the chaos of my life, God is forming, restoring, and redeeming. Praying the psalms is fully and completely God centered and eventually leads me to be joyful despite my circumstances.

Recognizing that I am a person who, to be joyful, needs all the help that's available, I'm always on the lookout for things that promote joy. An important source of help in this regard are the stories of people's lives. Countless biographies and autobiographies accompany me along the way. Several years ago a friend recommended *A Traveler Toward the Dawn: The Spiritual Journal of John Eagan, S.J.* It is the story of God's taking captive a man unknown to the wider world for whom "the manner was ordinary." And thus, John Eagan made an intimate relationship with God more accessible to ordinary folk.

In the book's introduction our eyes are opened to the ways we sabotage our own joy: "the point of John's journal is that we ourselves are the greatest obstacle to our own nobility of soul—which is what sanctity means. We judge ourselves unworthy servants, and as a result, our judgment becomes a self-fulfilling prophecy. We deem ourselves too inconsiderable to be used even by a God capable of miracles with no more than mud and spit. This false humility shackles an otherwise omnipotent God.

"John Eagan was not such a man."[11]

I've read this book countless times. Eagan has become like a close friend and "joy mentor" to me. He drank deeply from the well of God's joy. I like to believe John has shown me the way to that well and taught me how to drink from it. Now I don't want to spill a drop.

John Eagan died on Passion Sunday, April 12, 1987, only one

month after he was told he had terminal cancer. He was sixty-one years old. Only five days after his doctor told him of the cancer that was ravaging his body, he wrote a letter to his closest friends. In this letter he spoke of his relationship with God and the

> stronger and deeper attraction to the very Person of the Lord and a growing desire to be with him. Like a deep pull inside, an undertow…then the cancer thing comes along, and again, here is the Lord of my life moving in on me and telling me "Come home, John. I want you to be with me where I am. I want to share my joy, my love, and risen life with you. It will be grand, and it will be forever." And so deep down I feel myself saying, "Yes, let's go." I want to be with God.… Please pray that I may make this last journey in peace, in strong hope of the resurrection, and in growing desire to see face-to-Face this incomprehensible God to whom we give our lives.… Your prayer, your support and encouragement, and your humor in the days ahead will mean much to me.[12]

John Eagan, my brother, continues to encourage me to choose joy.

I've also discovered certain movies that connect me with the joy that sometimes becomes lost in the clutter of my life. One of my all-time favorites is *Patch Adams,* starring Robin Williams, based on the life of a doctor named Hunter Adams. In the opening scene, Hunter has admitted himself to a psychiatric hospital for depression and suicidal tendencies. As an attendant shows him to his room, another patient, an older man, approaches with four fingers extended into Hunter's face. The man screams, "How many fingers do you see?"

The attendant reproves the man, but the wild-eyed patient again pleads for Hunter's answer. "How many?"

Nervously, Hunter responds, "Four."

With outrage, the patient screams, "Four! Four! Another idiot!"

Later that evening Hunter goes to the old man's room and asks for an explanation. "Fingers," he says. "What's the answer?"

The older patient responds with sarcasm, then continues with some work at his desk. As he continues his work, Hunter notices that the man's paper coffee cup is leaking. So he silently repairs the leak with a piece of tape.

The man turns to face Hunter, extending four of Hunter's fingers. On screen, the older patient's face is the backdrop as Hunter looks at his own fingers.

"How many do you see?" the older man asks.

Nervously Hunter responds. "There are four out there."

"No! No! Look at me! You're focusing on the problem. If you focus on the problem, you can't see the solution. Look at me! How many do you see? Look beyond the fingers. How many do you see?"

As Hunter follows the directive, his fingers grow blurry and the patient's face comes into focus. At the same time, the blurry fingers appear to be eight rather than four.

Hunter nervously replies, "Eight."

The older patient jubilantly responds. "Eight! Eight! That's a good answer! See what no one else sees. See what everyone else chooses not to see out of fear of conformity or laziness.... Hunter, it looks like you are well on your way. You're going to see something here besides a crazy, bitter old man or you wouldn't have come here in the first place."

Wow. There is a brief, tender moment of silence as the two men look into each other's eyes. Then Hunter asks, "What do you see when you look at me, Arthur?"

After a pause, Arthur replies, "You fixed my cup.... I'll see you around...Patch." (Hence the nickname Patch Adams.)[13]

If I ever allow my troubles to become the focal point of my life, I will never see the opportunity for joy that every moment brings. Joy is always there beyond the hard things in life. The writer of Hebrews expresses, "Let us fix our eyes on Jesus ['How many fingers do you see?'], the author and perfecter of our faith, who for the joy set before him endured the cross, scorning its shame" (Hebrews 12:2, NIV). I can't help but wonder what Jesus' eyes were focused on while he hung on the cross for six hours. I imagine it wasn't the nails, the thorns, the spear, or his friends. I imagine he saw the face of his Father beyond the suffering.

For our joy to be real, it must somehow be congruous with the human condition and the realities of pain and sadness. Only the heart that has ached and known sorrow can fully know what experiencing joy really means.

JOY VERSUS HAPPINESS

Whenever things in my life leave me unhappy, joy can still be present because it comes from a different source. The word *happiness* comes from the same root as the word *happening,* which suggests that happiness is the result of something that happens to me. Happiness can be the result of my circumstances. If my family and friends treat me well, I'm happy. If my team wins the game, I'm happy. If I get the gift I hoped for, I'm happy.

Joy is something that confronts my circumstances and occurs in spite of sadness, difficulty, or loss. Happiness is a good feeling I get when things go a particular way; joy is an attitude I adopt in spite of how things go. Joy is a posture, a position; it's the deep assurance I have that the God who loves me is in control. Joy does not happen to me one day and avoid me the next. Joy is the result of a choice, a choice I have to make every day. It's a choice based on the knowledge that I belong to God, who is my Refuge. And nothing, not even death, can take God away from me.

I've wasted countless days caught in the trap of deferring joy until

I thought my circumstances had improved enough to warrant feeling joyful.

True joy is reserved for those who devote their lives to things that reach beyond their personal concerns and comfort. My friend Mark has invested the past twenty years working among the poor and homeless in Washington, D.C. One of my greatest concerns when he began this work was that he might become hard and cynical. On the contrary, rather than being overwhelmed with sorrow by the suffering around him, he glows with joy as he offers the love and mercy of God to those whom Jesus called "the least of these who are members of my family" (Matthew 25:40).

Mentors in Joy

Because we tend to become like the people we hang out with, it's essential that we befriend people who are joyful. Like most of the attitudes we adopt, joy is contagious. I have a friend who has loaned me some office space for many years. One of the things I appreciate even more than the free square footage is his joy. Wherever he goes and whomever he encounters, he is able to see and hear something positive, something for which he becomes joyful. My friend, Vic, is not blind to the sadness that surrounds him, but his spirit gravitates toward joy. His life reflects a rare faithfulness to Paul's exhortation, "whatever is true, whatever is honorable, whatever is just, whatever is pure, whatever is pleasing, whatever is commendable, if there is any excellence and if there is anything worthy of praise, think about these things" (Philippians 4:8). Vic's profound confidence in God allows him to know that faith is more real than doubt, hope more real than despair, and love more real than fear. His spiritual realism has made him a joyful man.

My maternal grandfather was a delightfully godly man but not in the typical, "churchy" sense of that word. I don't recall seeing him have a quiet time. The prayers I remember him offering before meals were of the common variety: "Come, Lord Jesus, our guest to be, and bless these gifts, bestowed by Thee…" I don't believe he ever attended a spiritual retreat. To my knowledge, he never read Christian books. Yet his joy and playfulness revealed a deep and enduring faith in God more than any other thing.

I cherish countless memories of his lightheartedness. He and I spent afternoons in the warehouse of his business playing hide and seek, eating candy together, and laughing. I remember him driving a car home one afternoon and inviting me to take a ride. Unaware that the passenger seat had been wired to mildly shock the passenger with a harmless jolt of electricity, I hopped inside. Driving down the street, my grandfather hit a switch, and the next thing I knew I was squealing, laughing, and begging him to stop. I recall one afternoon hurrying into the bathroom, lifting the toilet seat, and hearing a loud *pop* coming from a firework device he had attached to the toilet seat. My Papa loved to laugh and tease and surprise. I believe his smiles, and those he gave to others, caused God to smile too.

At his memorial service, the pastor referred to my Papa as the Candy Man. He explained that wherever my Papa went, he carried a big bag of candy to share with those he met along the way. My grandfather loved seeing others smile.

At the conclusion of the service, the pastor reminded us that our purpose had been to celebrate with gladness the memory of my Papa's life. He then announced that at the conclusion of the service he would stand at the exit and greet everyone with a big bag of candy. "When you pass, I want you to reach inside and grab a great big handful. Don't worry about how much you take, no one will be watching. Indulge yourself! It would make the Candy Man smile."

Another "joy mentor"[14] was my friend Bill, who today resides in a place of endless joy. At his memorial service, the pastor shared some words penned by Bill's granddaughter: "Never has anyone fascinated me so much as my granddad.... Granddad is never judgmental, but often is hilariously forthright and honest, telling things exactly as they are. He maintains a sense of humor that could never be matched; yet, his manners are never less than perfect. As music plays during the credits of a movie, he loves to step into the aisle and dance—something he does quite well. Everyone enjoys him." Indeed everyone did enjoy Bill, and as I remember his life today, my face is streaked with tears of joy.

While putting the finishing touches on this book's final chapter, I experienced a challenging slice of what life is all about. On a Saturday evening at summer's end, Lucie and I attended a fabulous outdoor wedding. The reception was held under a large tent on the bride's parents' front lawn. The food was wonderful, the music delightful, and the company of friends out of this world. It was a night filled with laughter and joy. But only a few days later, with the tent still standing, many of the same people who had celebrated the wedding there met again, this time to celebrate the life of a dear friend and entrust him to God's everlasting care. In many ways, it was a typical memorial service with music, prayers, Scripture readings, and a eulogy.

However, during the final half-hour, an invitation was extended to tell stories about Fred, who had been a special friend and neighbor of the bride's family. That's when the service became a celebration. Great sorrow and great joy arrived together as friends and family members stood and spoke of the life of this kind and caring man. I couldn't help but recall the words of Nehemiah to his grieving congregation: "the joy of the LORD is your strength" (Nehemiah 8:10) as I watched Fred's wife, Lynda, and his daughters, Juli and Carrie, gain strength from the joy that was expressed.

JOY OPENS THE HEART

When working with people who need God but don't acknowledge it, humor is a wonderful way to help them open their hearts. When

Christians invite others into their joy, laughter, and play, the message of Jesus' unconditional love is powerfully communicated. Countless times I've seen disinterested and joyless kids begin to laugh, and as they laughed, healing began.

One of the many highlights of my career in ministry to teenagers was a month spent at a Young Life resort where my good friend Bill (not the Bill mentioned before) and I were responsible for the program. For that month we took on the identity of two goofy characters, calling ourselves Ranger Guys and claiming sole responsibility for global management. Our uniforms consisted of khaki shorts and shirts, knee-socks, black patent-leather boots, and Mountie hats. Around our waists we wore utility belts that had attached to them a rotary-dial phone, turn-signal lights, a gallon-size gas container (marked HD GAS for "Highly Dangerous"), and various other items necessary for effective global management.

Every morning we greeted the campers with an outrageous explanation regarding things we had done to prepare for that day while they had been sleeping. "This morning we got up two hours before we went to bed, made twenty-one-speed bicycles out of pine needles, and rode them to the Grand Canyon, where we ran to the bottom and back with refrigerators strapped to our backs, filled with bowling balls, injected with lead (just to make them a little heavier), then sprinted twenty-two hundred miles back to camp. Now here we are refreshed and prepared to lead you Junior Rangers-in-Training through yet another day." Playful? Absolutely! Joyful? Without a doubt!

BIBLICAL PLAYFULNESS

Our absurd culture has made leisure a major industry, yet most of us know very little about playing. In fact, playfulness is a concept most of us don't easily welcome. To many people it sounds pointless and shallow, disruptive and irrelevant, ineffective and fruitless.

A dear friend's family is known for taking play to the next level. Nothing's more fun than packing the Suburban and its "activity capsule" with every game, toy, and swimming mask known to man and driving ten or twelve hours to their favorite beach. Long hours on the road produce gales of punch-drunk laughter over some goofy play on words or something funny that they saw earlier in the day. This is play in a pure form, a group effort that finds great joy in one another and in shared experiences.

Often what we refer to as play is laden with competition and compulsion. Many of us live for the weekend, since we think of play as the opposite of work—the after-work activities we engage in to recover, relax, and unwind. We approach play as something that enables us to return to work invigorated and renewed. Or maybe work is something we do that enables us to return to our play. Either way, this view of play turns it into work, which is not what God intended.

If I am to recover from my addiction to work and live a joyful life, play must take on its deeper meaning and become more than just a break from work. I want to embrace play and joy as a state of mind that reflects God's nature and character whether I'm working or doing something else. So often my spirit becomes heavy and my heart burdened because of a skewed perspective on life. It's a burden to believe that nothing is more important than my work. I'd be wise to learn from the angels who, I am told, can fly, not because they have wings, but because they have clearly seen God and thus take themselves lightly. I have the feeling that if I were to adopt their angelic attitude, I'd find myself better equipped to experience a holy playfulness, laughing robustly both in the good times and in the bad.

The concept of playfulness is biblically sound. The psalmist, for example wrote, "Be still, and know that I am God!" (Psalm 46:10). Don't overlook the fact that the Scriptures rarely contain exclamation marks! Another translation says, "Cease striving and know that I am God" (NASB). It has been suggested that both "be still" and "cease striving" really mean "have leisure." I think God is often saying to me, "Hey, Fil. It's time to play, kick back, and know that I am God."

PLAYING WITH GOD

Several years ago I directed a silent retreat with a small group on the East Coast. One of those attending, professor and author Dan Allender, openly acknowledged his reluctance to come, explaining he "didn't have the time or the desire to commune with God in silence, especially in the presence of others." To him, such an exercise seemed "not only pointless, but frivolous."[15] But at his wife's urging, he arrived at the retreat.

Writing about his experience later in his book *The Healing Path,* Dan indicated the silence was not as frightening as he had feared, yet he explained that his "mind felt caught between the sweetness of silence and the rising storm in my heart that seemed only to subside when I walked."[16] It was apparent that Dan was in a fight for his life. I observed him restlessly pacing the beach and moving from place to place within the house.

The final day of the retreat began with a meeting between just us two. He spoke of his experience the past two days: "I sank in fantasy, felt swarmed in worry, attacked by guilt, and devoured by emptiness." After listening for a while, I felt led to ask a single question: "Why are you so afraid to play with God?" Several of his stories had led to this bold query. It had become apparent that Dan was not comfortable with God or himself, least of all the two of them being together.

Upon hearing the question, he wrote later that he had experienced

a shudder that made me want to run out of the room either shrieking or dancing. I couldn't figure out what was gripping me.... When I left Fil, I walked first to the beach. "Play with God." Ridiculous. Pray, ponder, praise, produce for—yes. But play? I grew up fast and alone as an only child, and by an early age had become mostly destructive and antisocial. How could I play, and with God? He is not present, real, or fun. It dawned on me painfully: I didn't like God. I loved him, but I didn't like him. He was more like an articulate professor I wanted to learn from and then impress, but he surely wasn't a friend, and certainly not a playmate. But the Spirit urged me to play—not alone, but with the Trinity.[17]

He went on to express how the remainder of the day was too sacred for him to describe. "My greatest fear had been that if I availed myself to God, he would not show up. It became clear that my real fear was that I would not show up. When I did, he did in ways I relish."[18]

WHERE TO FROM HERE?

In most of our lives, happiness turns up, more or less, where we expect: a meaningful vocation, a fun vacation, or a good marriage. Largely, joy appears because of a particular kind of thinking, which leads to particular choices. "Cognitive psychologists remind us that always between the events that happen to us and our responses to them lie our *beliefs* or *interpretations* of those events."[19] This might explain the irrepressible joy found in the persons of faith we read about in the Scriptures. Those who believe the things God has said are not merely positive thinkers. Rather, they view every event in light of Jesus Christ's triumph over sin and death. They see the big picture. They know the outcome. And it brings them great joy.

Several years ago a dear friend's daughter was married in a beautiful, nearly perfect, wedding. The "nearly perfect" part had to do with the minister who had never presided over a wedding before. As the bride and her father approached the entrance to the sanctuary, they heard those familiar words most brides hear *after* their grand procession to the front of the sanctuary: "Dearly beloved, we are gathered together…" However, my friend and his daughter heard the words being spoken before they had taken even the first step down the aisle.

The bride immediately burst into tears. "Daddy, they began my wedding without me!" she cried. Calmly her dad patted her hand and reassuringly said, "It's all right, my little princess. This is a small matter. In twenty minutes, you'll be married! That's all that really matters." His words made her aware of a choice. She could choose to focus on the minister's blunder and be sad, or she could take delight in the truth that in twenty minutes the thing she had longed for more than a perfect wedding would have come true. She would be married to the love of her life.

Today, almost ten years later, what seemed to be the worst nightmare she would ever face has become a profound reminder that in the end, all that mattered was that on that day, in that church, the bride and groom became one.

Some would ask, "How in the world is it possible to be a joyful person in a pain-racked world where things fail to turn out as we hoped they would?" To others the answer is apparent. The basis for joy is a promise God made many centuries ago: "I'll marry you for good—forever! I'll marry you true and proper, in love and tenderness. Yes, I'll marry you and neither leave you nor let you go. You'll know me, GOD, for who I really am" (Hosea 2:19-20, MSG). If that's not reason enough, perhaps these words will help: "I've never quit loving you and never will. Expect love, love, and more love! (Jeremiah 31:3, MSG). Another promise that comes near the end of the Bible provides a further clue:

> Let us celebrate, let us rejoice,
> let us give him the glory!

The Marriage of the Lamb has come;
>   his Wife has made herself ready. (Revelation 19:7 MSG)

The good news the Bible presents is simple and clear. In the end, heaven's groom (Jesus) gets the bride (us).

The joy that is to come for all of God's people is so indescribable that the only image that can approach describing it is the joy between a lover and his or her beloved. The consummation of our union with God will be like a wedding of which the most beautiful, extravagant, and joyful wedding on earth offers only a faint foreshadowing.

———

On that day God will celebrate, dance, and eat fine food with his beloved sons and daughters. Our lifelong yearnings for intimacy will be fulfilled. It will be complete love with all of our heart's intensity. It will be total joy cascading over us. It will be forever. On that day the words of the prophet who attempted to express the inexpressible will be fulfilled:

So you'll go out in joy,
>   you'll be led into a whole and complete life.
The mountains and hills will lead the parade,
>   bursting with song.
All the trees of the forest will join the procession,
>   exuberant with applause. (Isaiah 55:12, MSG)

John the apostle did his best to speak the unspeakable too.

He will dwell with them as their God;
they will be his peoples,
and God himself will be with them;
he will wipe every tear from their eyes.

Death will be no more;

mourning and crying and pain will be no more,

for the first things have passed away. (Revelation 21:3-4)

For this reason, we can be joyful. In the end, God, you, and I will experience what our hearts have always longed for, and our hearts will be full of joy *forever.*

When I stopped running and started listening to God's whispering voice, I heard my true identity declared: "Fil, you're my beloved son, and I love you." Joy became the outcome, and I continue to learn this lesson.

As this final chapter draws to a close, I hope the story of God's relentless love for us and God's invitation for us to freely accept his indescribable love has shown that breakdowns in our lives can become breakthroughs. I have laid out my painful struggle with an addiction to work and busyness, hoping that it might help lead you toward the path of recovery. This path has led me to discover the powerful secrets provided by things such as solitude, prayer, sacred reading, spiritual direction, sorrow, and joy. You can discover those same secrets, for God longs for you to know him, to enjoy him, and to encounter him at the core of your being.

Now it's time for you and me to run. But not on empty.

—POINTS TO PONDER—

1. Who are your "joy mentors"? How can you arrange to spend more time with them to continue to be mentored in the life of joy?

2. If you have no joy mentors, think of a joyful person you know and invite him or her to have coffee or lunch with you this week.

3. "Do we imagine that when we step into a sailboat, God stays

ashore? Or that when we enter a movie, God waits on the sidewalk? Or that when we're in the heat of a tennis match, God is waiting in the church pew? We play, it is lovely, and we can revel in God in the midst of our play."[20] What thoughts or feelings do these words give rise to in your heart? Take time to write down the most meaningful and inspiring ideas that come to mind.

NOTES

Foreword

1. This quote is commonly attributed to Carl Jung although its source is not known.

Chapter 1

1. This description is based on information from a CNN News bulletin posted October 26, 1999, 03:13 A.M. Found at http://sports illustrated.cnn.com/golf/pga/news/1999/10/25/stewart_plane_ap/ index.html.

2. Found at http://www.lungusa.org/diseases/lungpneumoni.html.

3. See Sheldon Vanauken, *A Severe Mercy* (San Francisco: Harper & Row, 1977).

4. Thomas R. Kelly, *A Testament of Devotion* (New York: Harper & Row, 1941), 116.

Chapter 2

1. For more on this idea, see Thomas Merton, *The Wisdom of the Desert* (New York: New Directions, 1960), 3.

2. See Dallas Willard, *The Spirit of the Disciplines* (San Francisco: Harper & Row, 1988), 160.

3. Robert Benson, *Living Prayer* (New York: Tarcher/Putnam, 1998), 71.

4. C. S. Lewis, *The Lion, the Witch, and the Wardrobe* (New York: Religious Book Club, 1973), 29.

5. Søren Kierkegaard, *Purity of Heart Is to Will One Thing* (New York: Harper & Row, 1956), 107.

6. For more on the bane of efficiency, see Juliet Schor, *The Overworked American* (New York: Basic Books, 1993).

7. William Safire, "Too Much in Touch," *New York Times,* June 8, 2000.

8. Carl Jung, quoted in Morton T. Kelsey, *The Other Side of Silence: A Guide to Christian Meditation* (New York: Paulist Press, 1976), 83.

9. Barbara Walters and Ted Turner, quoted in Stephen Arterburn, *Winning at Work Without Losing at Love* (Nashville: Nelson, 1994), 141.

10. Maltbie D. Babcock, "This Is My Father's World."

11. Babcock, "This Is My Father's World."

12. Babcock, "This Is My Father's World."

13. Maltbie D. Babcock, "Be Strong."

14. The story of Maltbie Babcock was adapted from information found at www.cyberhymnal.org/bio/b/a/b/babcock_md.htm and www.acacia.pair.com/acacia.vignettes/Be.Strong.html and http://back tothebible.org/devotions/hymns_psalms/hymns.htm/207.

Chapter 3

1. Although a primary source that records this quote is elusive, Voltaire is widely credited with having spoken these words.

2. *The Big Kahuna,* dir. John Swanbeck, Lions Gate Films, 2000.

3. Frederick Buechner, *Whistling in the Dark* (San Francisco: HarperSanFrancisco, 1993), 105.

4. Parker Palmer, "The Monastic Way to Church Renewal: Borne Again," Saint Benedict Center's *Expressions* (January-February 1986). Parker Palmer is an activist, author, and teacher and was director of the resident program at the Saint Benedict Center.

5. German theologian Helmut Thielicke on Martin Luther, quoted in *Leadership Journal* (fall 1995): 86.

6. Samuel M. Lockeridge, quoted in Anne Graham Lotz, *Just Give Me Jesus* (Nashville: W Publishing Group, 2000), 1.

7. A. W. Tozer, *Knowledge of the Holy* (San Francisco: Harper & Row, 1961), 1.

Chapter 4

1. See Mark 5:1-20.

2. Evelyn Underhill, *The Spiritual Life* (Harrisburg, Pa.: Morehouse, 1994), 20.

Chapter 5

1. C. S. Lewis, *The Screwtape Letters* (New York: HarperCollins, 1942), 63-7.

2. Robert Benson, *Living Prayer* (New York: Tarcher/Putnam, 1998), 89. This prayer is adapted from the 1979 edition of *The Book of Common Prayer.*

3. Benson, *Living Prayer,* 97-8.

4. *Bedazzled,* dir. Harold Ramis, 20th Century Fox Film Corporation, 2000.

5. See John 4:32.

6. I was reminded of this list when I read Howard Baker's book *Soul Keeping* (Colorado Springs: NavPress, 1998), 32.

7. Parker Palmer, "The Monastic Way to Church Renewal: Borne Again," Saint Benedict Center's *Expressions* (January-February 1986).

8. Sue Monk Kidd, *When the Heart Waits* (San Francisco: HarperCollins, 1990), 22.

9. Frederick Buechner, *Whistling in the Dark* (San Francisco: HarperSanFrancisco, 1993), 108.

Chapter 6

1. Sam Walter Foss, "The Prayer of Cyrus Brown," in *Stars to Steer By,* ed. Louis Untermeyer (New York: Harcourt Brace, 1941), 301-2.

2. Dom Chapman, quoted in Richard Foster, *Prayer: Finding the Heart's True Home* (New York: HarperCollins, 1992), 7.

3. Jean-Nicholas Grou, *How to Pray,* trans. Joseph Dalby (Greenwood, S.C.: Attic, 1982), 18.

4. George Bernard Shaw, *Saint Joan,* as quoted in a sermon preached at the Village Chapel, Pinehurst, N.C., December 8, 2002, by Larry H. Ellis.

5. George Arthur Buttrick, *Prayer* (New York: Abingdon-Cokesbury, 1942), 233-4.

6. For more on the prayers of these biblical figures, see the following passages: Jeremiah (Jeremiah 18:20), Nehemiah (Nehemiah 1:4), Abraham (Genesis 17:3), Daniel (Daniel 6:10), Ezekiel (Ezekiel 11:13), Hannah (1 Samuel 1:13), Moses (Exodus 20:1–24:2), the blind beggar (Mark 10:47), Peter (Acts 9:40; Matthew 14:30), Paul

(1 Corinthians 14:15), David (Psalm 5:3), Job (the entire book of Job chronicles his prayers of complaint to God), Mary (Luke 1:46-55), Jonah (Jonah 2:1), Anna (Luke 2:37). I also enthusiastically recommend reading *Prayer: Finding the Heart's True Home* by Richard Foster (HarperCollins), *Between Heaven and Earth: Prayers and Reflections that Celebrate an Intimate God* by Ken Gire (HarperCollins).

Chapter 7

1. Vincent van Gogh, his fourteenth letter to his sister Wilhelmina (Wil), from Saint-Rémy, September 19, 1889. This and other letters are found at http://www.vangoghgallery.com/letters/to_wil.htm.

2. I am deeply grateful to Ken Gire for his chapter on Scripture in his book *Windows of the Soul: Experiencing God in New Ways* (Zondervan, 1996).

3. Van Gogh to his sister, September 19, 1889.

4. Henry Scougal, quoted in Kenneth Boa, *Sacred Readings* (Colorado Springs: NavPress, 2000), 7.

5. Martin Luther, quoted in Michael Green, ed., *Illustrations for Biblical Preaching* (Grand Rapids: Baker, 1989), 35.

6. Theonas of Alexandria, *The Epistle of Theonas,* quoted in Timothy Jones, gen. ed., *The Spiritual Formation Bible* (Grand Rapids: Zondervan, 1999), 287.

7. The desert father John Cassian first introduced the ancient art of spiritual reading, also referred to as *lectio divina,* early in the fifth century. The sixth-century Rule of Saint Benedict that gave form and substance to the monastic practice outlined a plan for daily periods of spiritual reading. In recent years writers like Thomas Merton *(Contemplative Prayer, New Seeds of Contemplation, Spiritual Direction & Meditation),* Thomas Keating *(Intimacy with God, Open Mind, Open Heart),* Eugene Peterson *(Working the Angles),* Thelma Hall *(Too Deep for Words),* Robert Mulholland *(Shaped by the Word),* Kenneth Boa *(Sacred Readings),* and Susan Muto *(A Practical Guide to Spiritual Reading)* have provided excellent resources and wonderful companions as you travel toward this practice.

8. Thomas à Kempis, *Imitation of Christ* (New York: Grosset & Dunlap, *n.d.*), 10. Here I have taken the liberty of adapting some of the language to make it more readable and understandable.

9. Madame Guyon, *Madame Guyon: Experiencing the Depths of Jesus Christ* (Goleta, Calif.: Christian Books, 1975), 16.

10. Thomas Merton, *New Seeds of Contemplation* (New York: New Directions, 1961), 224.

11. Merton, *New Seeds of Contemplation*, 6.

Chapter 8

1. Anne Tyler, *Morgan's Passing* (New York: Ballantine Books, 1980), 3-21; 122-31.

2. In my friend Brennan Manning's powerful book *The Ragamuffin Gospel: Good News for the Bedraggled, Beat-Up, and Burnt Out* (Portland, Oreg.: Multnomah, 1990), 197, Manning explains the origin and use of the phrase: "Over a hundred years ago in the Deep South, a phrase so common in our Christian culture today, *born again,* was seldom or never used. Rather, the phrase used to describe the breakthrough into a personal relationship with Jesus Christ was, 'I was seized by the power of a great affection.'"

3. Some of the most significant books that helped change the direction of my spiritual life were *Celebration of Discipline: The Path to Spiritual Growth* by Richard Foster; *A Testament of Devotion* by Thomas R. Kelly; *Beginning to Pray* by Anthony Bloom; *Spiritual Friend: Reclaiming the Gift of Spiritual Direction* by Tilden Edwards; *The Practice of the Presence of God* by Brother Lawrence; *Group Spiritual Direction: Community for Discernment* by Rose Mary Dougherty; *Soul Friend: The Practice of Christian Spirituality* by Kenneth Leech; and *Spiritual Direction and Meditation* by Thomas Merton.

4. Henri Nouwen, *The Genesee Diary: Report from a Trappist Monastery* (Garden City, N.Y.: Image Books, 1981), 13.

5. Tilden Edwards, *Spiritual Friend: Reclaiming the Gift of Spiritual Direction* (Ramsey, N.J.: Paulist, 1980), 133-73, offers a tremendous wealth of wisdom and information. I will be forever in the debt of Tilden Edwards, Rose Mary Dougherty, Gerald May, and their staff for their mentoring during my two-year involvement in the Shalem Institute Program in Christian Spiritual Guidance.

6. Saint Benedict, *The Rule of St. Benedict,* chap. 53, quoted in Joan Chittister, *Wisdom Distilled from the Daily: Living the Rule of St. Benedict Today* (New York: HarperCollins, 1991), 121. Chapter 10 in this book offers a helpful and practical explanation of hospitality as it is practiced in the Benedictine tradition.

7. Brennan Manning, *Abba's Child: The Cry of the Heart for Intimate Belonging* (Colorado Springs: NavPress, 1994), 55-6.

8. Saint Bernard (Epistle 87, no. 7), found at http://www.shrineof saintjude.net/home2401.html.

9. Friedrich von Hügel, quoted in Jerome M. Neufelder and Mary C. Coelho, eds., *Writings on Spiritual Direction by Great Christian Masters* (New York: Seabury Press, 1982), 8.

Chapter 9

1. See Matthew 27:46 and Mark 15:34, which echo the cry heard in Psalm 22:1-2.

2. John 8:32, NIV.

3. Viktor Frankl, *Man's Search for Meaning,* 3d ed. (New York: Simon and Schuster, 1984), 86-7.

4. C. S. Lewis, *The Problem of Pain* (New York: HarperCollins, 2001), 91.

5. A. W. Tozer, *God Tells the Man Who Cares* (Camp Hill, Pa.: Christian Publications, 1992).

6. Brother André, quoted by Daniel F. McSheffer, "Brother André: Montreal's Miracle Man. Found at www.catholic.net/rcc/ Periodicals/Homiletic?07-97/andre/html.

7. Emily Dickinson, "A Great Hope Fell," in *The Complete Poems of Emily Dickinson,* ed. Thomas H. Johnson (Boston: Little, Brown, 1961), 504.

8. Craig Barnes, *Yearning: Living Between How It Is and How It Ought to Be* (Downers Grove, Ill.: InterVarsity, 1991), 27. I am deeply indebted to Craig Barnes for the wisdom he has passed on in this and his other work, *When God Interrupts* (InterVarsity Press).

9. Oswald Chambers, *My Utmost for His Highest* (Uhrichsville, Ohio: Barbour, 1963), 211.

Chapter 10

1. John Ortberg, *The Life You've Always Wanted* (Grand Rapids: Zondervan, 1997), 65.

2. G. K. Chesterton, *Orthodoxy* (San Francisco: Ignatius Press, 1995), 66.

3. Henry Van Dyke, "Joyful, Joyful, We Adore Thee," in *The Poems of Henry Van Dyke* (New York: Charles Scribner's Sons, 1911), quoted in *Hymns for the Family of God* (Nashville: Paragon Associates, 1976), 377.

4. C. S. Lewis, *Letters to Malcolm: Chiefly on Prayer* (New York: Harcourt, Brace & World, 1964), 93.

5. Ortberg, *The Life You've Always Wanted,* 68.

6. Ortberg, *The Life You've Always Wanted,* 67.

7. Michael Yaconelli, *Dangerous Wonder: The Adventure of Childlike Faith* (Colorado Springs: NavPress, 1998), 66-7.

8. Yaconelli, *Dangerous Wonder,* 67.

9. James Joyce, *A Portrait of the Artist As a Young Man* (New York: Viking, 1956), 154-5.

10. Frances de Sales, *Introduction to a Devout and Holy Life* (New York: Doubleday, 1989), 254.

11. John Eagan, *A Traveler Toward the Dawn: The Spiritual Journal of John Eagan, S.J.,* ed. William J. O'Malley (Chicago: Loyola Press, 1990), xii.

12. Eagan, *A Traveler Toward the Dawn,* 1-3.

13. *Patch Adams,* dir. Tom Shadyac, Universal Pictures, 1998.

14. I am grateful to John Ortberg for his introduction of the term "joy mentor." His writing on the subject of joy has been tremendously meaningful and helpful to me.

15. Dan Allender, *The Healing Path* (Colorado Springs: WaterBrook Press, 1999), 203.

16. Allender, *The Healing Path,* 203.

17. Allender, *The Healing Path,* 204.

18. Allender, *The Healing Path,* 204.

19. Ortberg, *The Life You've Always Wanted,* 78.

20. Marilyn Gustin, *We Can Know God* (Liguori, Mo.: Liguori Publications, 1993), 120.

ABOUT THE AUTHOR

Fil Anderson speaks at conferences and leads retreats throughout the United States. He lives with his wife, Lucie, and their three children in Greensboro, North Carolina.

He can be reached by mail at

Journey Resources
P. O. Box 9801
Greensboro, NC 27429